THE GARDENS OF BRITAIN 1

GENERAL EDITOR: John Sales, Gardens Adviser, National Trust

By the same author

MOUNTAINS OF THE MOON
BORNEO JUNGLE (With Tom Harrisson and others)
PLANTS WITH PERSONALITY
A DIVERSITY OF PLANTS
A DICTIONARY OF GARDEN PLANTS IN COLOUR (with Roy Hay)
A DICTIONARY OF ROSES IN COLOUR (with S. Millar Gault)
IN SEARCH OF FLOWERS
FLOWERS AND COLOUR IN WINTER

As part editor

THE ROYAL HORTICULTURAL SOCIETY DICTIONARY OF
    GARDENING AND ITS SUPPLEMENTS
GREAT FLOWER BOOKS

Devon and Cornwall

Patrick M. Synge VMH

In association with the
Royal Horticultural Society

B.T. Batsford Ltd *London*

Dedicated in gratitude to the makers of some of the outstanding gardens of the South-West, to whom we owe so much and who were responsible for introducing and raising so many good plants and whose gardens are now open at times for us to enjoy and learn from; in particular to

Lt Col Sir Edward Bolitho of Trengwainton
Mr George H. Johnstone of Trewithen
Mr Augustus Smith of Tresco Abbey
Mr John Charles Williams of Caerhays Castle

First published 1977
Second impression 1978

© Patrick M. Synge 1977

ISBN 0 7134 0927 4

Filmset in 10 on 12pt. Photina by
Servis Filmsetting Ltd, Manchester

Printed in Great Britain by
The Anchor Press Ltd
and bound by
Wm Brendon & Son Ltd
both of Tiptree, Essex
for the publishers
B. T. Batsford Ltd
4 Fitzhardinge Street,
London W1H 0AH

Contents

List of Illustrations   6

List of Colour Plates   8

List of Garden Plans   9

Acknowledgments   9

Map of the Gardens of Devon and Cornwall   10

Introduction   13

The Gardens of Devon   19

The Gardens of Cornwall   83

Some Other Gardens Open to the Public   146

Index   149

List of Illustrations

(All illustrations are between pages 96 and 97)

1   Bicton, Nr Budleigh Salterton. Part of the formal Italianate Garden.
2   Part of the Pinetum at Bicton.
3   Cotehele. The old dovecote with ornamental pond beside.
4   Castle Hill, Nr Barnstaple. Part of the view from the front of the house showing one of the stone lions and also a very good urn.
5   Endsleigh. The terrace designed by Humphry Repton.
6   Endsleigh. Nr Tavistock. A tall weeping beech in the arboretum.
7   Endsleigh. *Pinus montezumae*.
8   The Garden House, Buckland Monachorum. *Clematis indivisa*, from New Zealand. A rare clematis to see outside even in a sheltered corner.
9   Buckland. Part of the old tower and the lowest herbaceous and shrub border.
10 Killerton. Trunks of the surviving cork oak, *Quercus suber*.
11 Killerton. *Magnolia kobus* hybrid near the entrance.
12 Knightshayes Court, Nr Tiverton. The long walk with raised beds for choice alpines.
13 Knightshayes. The pool garden.
14 Marwood Hill, Nr Barnstaple. Part of one of the pools with the bank leading up to the wall behind. Pampas grass makes a fine focal point reflected in the water.
15 Saltram. Part of the avenue. It is underplanted with old daffodils for flower in spring and cyclamen in autumn. At the end is a Turkey Oak.
16 Sharpitor. Part of the *Magnolia campbellii* in flower in March.
17 Antony House. Looking towards the house from the end of the lawn.
18 *Carya ovata*, the Shagbark hickory, an old and rarely seen tree on the lawn at Antony House.

19   Carclew Garden, between Truro and Falmouth. Old rhodo-
     dendrons. In the foreground *Rhododendron falconeri*, a large-
     leaved species probably grown from Sir Joseph Hooker's
     original seed.

20   Carclew Garden. Old 'Cornish Red' rhododendrons around
     ornamental pond and in fountain.

21   Looking down on old rhododendrons at Carclew.

22   Glendurgan. *Agave americana* with flower spike on lawn.
     Mrs Helen Fox, the former owner of the garden, stands beside
     it.

23   **Glendurgan. A very old tulip tree in spring showing rhodo-
     dendrons behind and bluebells below.**

24   Lamellen, Nr Wadebridge, a garden where many good
     rhododendrons were raised. The light one is called 'Lamellen'
     after the garden.

25   Tremeer, St Tudy. A garden where General Harrison has
     specialised in raising bright violet blue rhododendrons. He
     also grows camellias in large quantities. 'Donation' is shown
     on the right.

26   Lanhydrock House. Tree magnolias in flower on the hillside.

27   Penjerrick House. Here many famous rhododendrons were
     raised including 'Penjerrick' and 'Cornish Cross'. A fine
     weeping beech is in the background.

28   Trengwainton House. A veteran tree of *Rhododendron
     falconeri*.

29   Tresco Abbey, Isles of Scilly. Part of the Palm Walk, leading
     up to the Neptune Steps. A fine *Furcrea bedinghausii* is in
     flower on left, in centre two royal palms and on right the
     mass of *Metrosideros tomentosa*, the rata of New Zealand.

30   Trewithen. Top of the great lawn looking away from the
     house.

31   **Trewithen. *Rhododendron macabeanum*, by many considered
     the finest specimen in the country. The flower is a deep
     yellow.**

The Colour Plates

1   *Magnolia campbellii* in full bloom in early March at Sharpitor, Salcombe. The chief glory of this interesting garden.
2   An unusual hybrid of *Rhododendron williamsianum* near entrance at The Garden House, Buckland Monachorum, Nr Tavistock.
3   *Erythronium revolutum* in the Woodland Garden of Knightshayes Court, Nr Tiverton.
4   The top of *Magnolia sargentiana robusta* showing an abundance of flower at Caerhays Castle, Cornwall.
5   *Eucalyptus ficifolia* at Tresco Abbey, Isle of Scilly.
6   The trunks of *Myrtus luma* at Tresco Abbey, Isle of Scilly.
7   A truss of *Rhododendron macabeanum* on the great tree at Trewithen, Grampound Road, Cornwall.

List of Garden Plans

	page
Gardens of Devon and Cornwall	10–11
Bicton Gardens	24–25
Dartington Hall	34–35
The Garden House, Buckland Monachorum	50
Knightshayes Court	60–61
Trengwainton	124–125
Tresco Abbey Gardens	136–137

ACKNOWLEDGMENTS

The Author and Publisher would like to thank F. Naylor: colour plates 5 and 6
Harry Smith Collection: colour plate 7
A.G. Murdoch: colour plate 1
The monochrome illustrations are from the author's collection

9

CORNWALL

1 Antony
2 Caerhayes
3 Carclew
4 Chyverton
5 County Demonstration Garden
6 Glendurgan
7 Ince
8 Lamellen
9 Lanhydrock
10 Pencarrow
11 Penjerrick
12 St. Michael's Mount
13 Trelissick
14 Tremeer
15 Trengwainton
16 Trerice*
17 Tresco
18 Trewithen

DEVON

1 Arlington Court
2 Bicton
3 Blackpool House*
4 Castle Drogo
5 Castle Hill
6 Combe Head*
7 Dartington Hall
8 Endsleigh
9 Flete
10 Garden House
11 Killerton
12 Knightshayes
13 Marwood Hill
14 Metcombe Brake
15 Powys
16 Rosemoor
17 Saltram
18 Sharpitor
19 Slade
20 Staplers*
21 Tapeley Park*
22 Woodside*

C O R N W

Bodmin

Newquay

St Austell

Truro

Falmouth

Penzance

THE SCILLY ISLES

* These garde

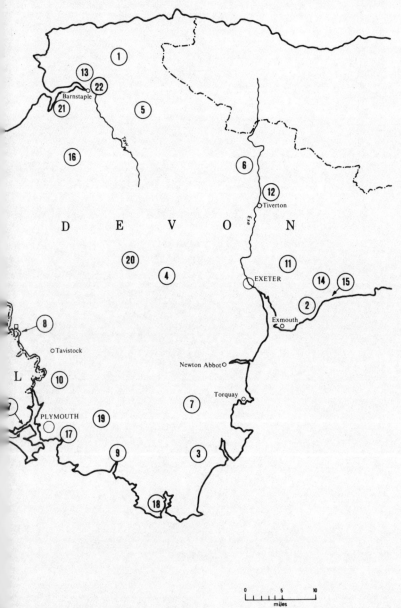

and in the list on pages 146 and 147.

Introduction

The gardens of Devon and Cornwall, these are magical words conjuring up not only vast rhododendrons, camellias and magnolias, the sub-tropical island of Tresco, with its strange plants, gardens specially favoured by the sea, but also gardens high upon the moorland and exposed to every wind. It was a tempting assignment to write about them. I have enjoyed it. These gardens are so varied and so rich in their plants and they have such a long season of flowering throughout the year. I confess that I am not a Devonian or a Cornishman but a detached view is sometimes helpful.

Probably there is no area in the world where a greater variety of plants can be grown and have been grown. We owe much to the great gardeners of Devon and Cornwall who supported the fervent plant collectors, such as Forrest, Wilson and Kingdon Ward, took infinite trouble to raise and prick out the seedlings, extending their grounds into the woods to accommodate them, and built up such splendid gardens. Places like Caerhays, Trewithen, Antony House, Trengwainton, Tresco and Knightshayes are never likely to be repeated and they are all now open for you to enjoy. From many of them you can even go away with choice plants for your own garden. They are gardens for everyone, not only for the friends of the owner. Seeing them has encouraged gardeners to be bolder in their planting. Gardens in Sussex such as Nymans and Wakehurst and the Savill Gardens of Windsor Great Park have shown that the great magnolias of the Yulan section such as M. campbellii will flower there as well, and how magnificent they are! Thousands of their huge pink flowers standing up against the blue sky, each one breathtaking in its beauty of form and, in the mass, staggering. Then think of the hundreds of trusses of Rhododendron macabeanum at Trewithen, deep yellow in flower against its dark green foliage. Certainly size of plant is one of the things we associate with gardens in Devon and Cornwall, often larger and growing better than they grow in their native Sino-Himalayan or South American forests. If only the collectors Hooker, Forrest, Lobb – a Cornishman – and

13

Comber could see now what they had brought us.

Devon and Cornwall gardens were mostly designed for spring effect and concentrated on plants that flower then. In summer the owners went off to Scotland. This is changed now. Great crowds come in summer and want to see colour. The gardens have adapted to this without losing their spring magnificence; hydrangeas are the great standby. They do particularly well by the sea and like the moisture-laden air. They are also wind resistant. At Trengwainton, near Penzance, we can see a great collection, and another is at Trelissick. *Viburnum betulifolium* makes an absolute cascade of scarlet berries each autumn at Trewithen, while in other gardens there are carpets of *Cyclamen neapolitanum*, such a good plant since with foliage and flower it pays rent for nine months of the year and only needs an annual mulch of leaf mould in July. Fuchsias have been planted more and are valuable while the hardy *F. magellanica* has naturalised as hedges near the sea. The Hebes, the shrubby veronicas, make valuable foliage and flower effects.

The first thing on which the gardens depend is wind shelter, especially near the coast; without it few things will grow well. That is why many of the larger gardens are woodland ones. Also such conditions suit the camellias, rhododendrons and magnolias as long as the trees are suitably thinned. The best trees and bushes for providing wind shelter are curiously not native ones, although the sycamore and the ash are better than the oak or beech. *Pinus radiata*, the Monterey pine from California is very fast growing and wind resistant. Majestic trees can be grown in half a lifetime. The late Mr Arnold Foster of Eagle's Nest, Zennor lived in a very exposed place facing the Atlantic, but it was relatively mild and in his book *Shrubs for the Milder Counties*, he shows us what can be grown. It is now out of print but for anyone starting a garden in Devon or Cornwall it is well worth searching the second hand shops for a copy. Such plants as *Olearia albida* with grey foliage, *Senecio rotundifolius*, the Pittosporums such as *P. tobira* and *P. tenuifolium* in its varieties are all from overseas but all worth growing in such situations. Escallonias are also very tough and *E.macrantha* makes an unrivalled hedge near the sea. Down by the South Coast of the Lizard mesembryanthemums and *Carpobrotus*, the large fleshy 'mesembryanthemum', have spread freely over the rocks and survive the winters. The Isles of Scilly and in particular Tresco Abbey Gardens are like another and a strange world full of pelargoniums from South Africa, *Furcraeas*, 8 ft tall with spires of flower like cascading showers of green from South America, *Banksias* from Australia, and *Metrosideros* from New Zealand, so vast that its red flower mass can be seen from out at sea.

The majority of the soils are acid and have built up accumulations of leafmould over the years. The moorlands of Exmoor and Dartmoor are both very acid and the water draining down towards the coast tends to bring acidity with it. Peat is present naturally in many areas. Clays are also present but the effect is often masked by the masses of leafmould accumulated above. The rocks, often close to the surface, are shaly and tend to break up quickly and the soils derived from them are usually stony and well-drained. In other areas the prevailing rock is granitic and harder. The majority of the great gardens are near the coast where the climate is milder than in the centre. Gardens of the coast have an appreciably higher rainfall than those further inland and much more than those in the more Eastern counties. It is also appreciably milder as regards hard frosts although I can remember feeling very cold in early spring in some of them. The humidity is generally high. There are a few areas mainly nearer the eastern parts of the counties where the soil is slightly alkaline but they do not hold the great gardens and I do not recollect visiting any where they could not grow rhododendrons or camellias. It is usually so moist that rhododendrons flourish as probably they have done nowhere else. In the spring and early summer they make a great show, both species and the beautiful hybrids raised both in Devon and in Cornwall. One thinks of 'Cornish Cross' and 'Penjerrick' raised at Penjerrick, still in the front rank of hybrids, of 'Red Admiral' that early flowering giant raised at Caerhays. The raising of hybrids is still continuing: the brilliant violet blues from Tremeer raised by General Eric Harrison and named after Cornish Saints, 'St Breward', 'St Tudy' and 'St Minver'. Then there are the tender sweet-scented *Maddeniis* with flowers like white lily trumpets. *R.lindleyi*, *R.taggianum* and for specially sheltered spots the enormous flowers of *R.nuttallii* and its fine hybrid 'Tyermannii'. In many gardens the delicately scented hybrids 'Lady Alice Fitzwilliam' and 'Fragrantissimum' have made great clumps to be measured in yards across with billowing masses of white trumpets.

The plants from South America have flourished equally, the eucryphias from Chile, so valuable for their summer flowering and the *Crinodendrons* with their hanging crimson lanterns all over the bush. *C.hookeranum* is the plant that was formerly called *Tricuspidaria lanceolata* and is often so known. Then the Chilean fire bush *Embothrium coccineum* is a flaming mass of orange red in May nearly every year. No tree surpasses it for brightness. The Southern beeches, the Nothofagus from both Chile and New Zealand have added very fast growing and graceful trees to rival our European beeches. The exoticism that we associate with tropical gardens is here in the tree ferns *Dicksonia antarctica* from New Zealand, and *Phormium tenax* with its leaves like 6 foot swords, also from New Zealand, and *Cordyline australis* and the wider-leaved, but more tender, *C.indivisa* which has more colour in the leaves. These take the place of the palm in a Riviera garden.

I urge you to go and visit these gardens, take note of when they are open from the *National Trust Guide*, the yellow book of *Gardens Open under the National Gardens Scheme*, the *Gardeners Sunday Booklet, Historic Houses, Castles and Gardens* guide and the little booklet of *Gardens Open* issued by the Cornwall Garden Society. It is not too early to go in March to some of them, while April and May are the peak months for the magnolias, the camellias and the rhododendrons. An early spring garden visiting tour in Devon and Cornwall will be very rewarding and the roads will be pleasant and far less crowded than in July and August. September is another good time to go for the hydrangeas. I hope that this book may encourage you. It only mentions a proportion of the plants to be seen. By necessity it is full of Latin names since the plants have in most cases no others but even if one does not take down the names and cannot hope to plant so widely in one's own garden there is still so much to be learned and so much beauty to be absorbed. There are a few houses of great artistic or historic interest or formal layout. Most date from the middle of the last century or from the early years of this one. Their history lies in the plants they have raised and grown. Some of the houses such as Antony, Dartington, Ince, Pencarrow and Trewithen are older and have great architectural merit as well as interesting collections of pictures and furniture to complement the gardens.

We should indeed feel grateful to the great gardeners who made them and who encouraged plant collectors to brave journeys in distant and difficult parts to bring back seeds (often their journeys lasted years, not weeks); then to their children and to their successors who have carried them on, often with little help with their labour.

In particular I would like to thank the many owners and gardeners who have entertained my wife and me so hospitably, given freely of their time in showing us round and answering our questions. It is difficult to pick out a few but I would like to mention particularly Mr and Mrs Ambrose Baker who accompanied us for part of our tour, Lady Amory of Knightshayes, the late Mrs George Johnstone of Trewithen, Sir John and the late Lady Carew Pole of Antony House, Major Simon Bolitho of Trengwainton, Lord and Lady Boyd of Ince Castle, Sir John and Mrs Molesworth St Aubyn of Pencarrow, The Hon J.F. and Mrs St Aubyn of St Michael's Mount, Mr and Mrs Lionel Fortescue of the Garden House, Major E.W.M. Magor of Lamellen, Mrs Fox of Glendurgan, Col. and the Lady Anne Palmer of Rosemoor, Mr and Mrs Nigel Holman of Chyverton and Dr J.A. Smart of Marwood Hill. In many cases they have also read my scripts and made helpful suggestions. My wife has nobly undertaken the preparation of the Index and in so doing pointed out many small corrections and improvements and I am very grateful. Mrs Julet Tuck typed most of the MS for me with great expertise.

The conservation of these gardens, both large and small is a constant difficulty. They are always changing, and replacements and new plants are required. A few great gardens, alas, are no longer being kept up and have gone out of the list. Your visits can encourage the owners, but respect their gardens and try and do no damage. Some places now sell plants and it is encouraging to them if you buy something, also, in years to come, it may be infinitely rewarding to you. The list is constantly changing, some may go out while others will come in, therefore I have dealt especially with those preserved by the National Trust and other bodies. I have not been able to see or to include every garden that is open but the lists of the National Gardens Scheme will keep you up to date. Some of these may indeed be beautiful and well worth visiting and I apologise to those gardeners whose gardens have not been included. I shall be glad to hear from them in case there should be future amended editions of this book.

The conditions for inclusion as set by the publishers for this series included firstly the agreement of the owner and secondly that at the time of writing the garden was open to the public on at least one day a year.

The Gardens of Devon

Arlington Court

The National Trust

On east side of A39 Barnstaple to Lynton Road, 7 miles NW of Barnstaple, entrance well signposted from A39. Bequeathed to National Trust in 1949 by Miss Rosalie Chichester. Garden and park open daily throughout year. April to 31 October 11 am–1 pm and 2–6 pm. House also open. Soil sandy and acid overlying granite. Altitude 900 feet above sea level. Rainfall 55 in. with much damp mist.

Arlington Court is the highest garden in Devon belonging to the National Trust and being only about 5 miles from the North Devon coast and standing on high ground is exposed to strong gales from the west. The park was planted in early Victorian times and in spite of the wind has some fine trees and also vast clumps of rhododendrons, mostly old hybrids of *R.arboreum* such as 'Altaclarense' which received an award from the Royal Horticultural Society in 1865 and the purple-flowered *R.ponticum*. One of these on the edge of the main lawn measured a quarter of an acre in extent until recently some of the centre was cut out. Opposite the front door is a vast Turkey oak probably over 100 feet tall and more across and also the biggest *Quercus ilex*, the evergreen oak, that I have ever seen, almost as tall. It is probably the variety *latifolia* which is more tender and with looser more attractive growth than the one usually seen. These are probably about 100 years old. On the other side of the lawn are two large variegated sycamores, a form rarely seen.

Miss Chichester was a nature conservationist and when the National Trust took over the estate, the park, which is very large and spacious, was much overgrown, the lawns being chiefly mown by rabbits. One corollary of this is the wild flowers which had spread among the grass and naturalised, the blue speedwell *Veronica persica*, still flowering freely where the grass is not trimmed short, *Claytonia siberica* under the sycamores, primroses of varying colour and candelabra primulas. These last have diminished as the grass has been cut shorter but efforts are being made to increase them again. In general it is a fine example of early Victorian planting on a spacious scale deriving its effect from its great oaks, sycamores and beeches and the lovely views between them. The National Trust had much to do when they took over and have done some planting of young trees but have preserved the general effect. One of the interesting features is a collection of the species and varieties of *Fraxinus*, the ash. Another unusual tree to the left of the path around the front lawn is a holly *Ilex dipyrena* about 100 years old.

On the left also one comes to the Victorian gardens which are terraced in three levels but have been much simplified over the years. A wide path leads up to a round pond with two iron herons each standing on one leg. The heron was the crest of the Chichester family. Flanking it are two large old monkey puzzle trees and two small ones have been planted beside, eventually to replace them. At the top flanked by a high wall is a decorative Victorian conservatory which is not at present open and may later need replacement. A high wall with climbers flanks the conservatory and in front of these are two broad herbaceous borders which are colourful during the late summer. At the right hand end of the border is a decorative arch with wisteria. In September masses of *nerines bowdenii*, the Guernsey lily, flower with tall pink heads. The lower border is shaped as a rock bank with early flowering bulbs and alpine plants. Here Queen Anne's double jonquil *Narcissus eystettensis* has spread freely and flowers in early to mid April. It is very rarely seen in such large clumps.

On the left as one walks up the steps an unusually large *Cupressus macrocarpa* with several trunks, probably about 80 feet tall, is notable and is one of the largest trees in the Park.

Returning to the main path one comes to St James's Church and a large pond in which its tower is reflected. Here are some interesting moisture-loving spreading plants such as *Polygonum* and *Fagopyrum*. Near here also are the stables with the famous collection of old carriage vehicles. It is possible to take a ride round the estate at regular intervals and this is an excellent way to see it. There is also an interesting nature trail starting from a style near the end of the ha-ha by a large horse chestnut at the corner of the lawn and also more groups of rhododendrons and azaleas. Notable in April was a large deep crimson hybrid of *R.thomsonii* and groups of pale yellow *R.lutescens*. In autumn the colour is provided by masses of hydrangeas. The rhododendron lover should also visit the main drive through the Lodge Plantation marked on the sketch map in the guide. There are no new plantings here but some of the older ones such as the large-leaved *R.falconeri* have reached a good size. In clearings in the grass are masses of candelabra primulas at their best in May.

Bicton Gardens and Pinetum

Lord Clinton

At East Budleigh, near Budleigh Salterton. Entrance from A376 on the Budleigh Salterton–Newton Poppleford road. Only 1½ miles from sea and about equidistant between Exmouth and Sidmouth. Gardens and Pinetum open daily from end March–end October. 10 am–5.30 pm. House, now an agricultural and horticultural College, not open. A fine Italian garden and a Pinetum containing one of the finest collections of conifers in the country. Plants for sale in garden shop near entrance. Restaurant. Soil light fertile loam overlying sandstone, acid. Rainfall average 34.5 in.

Bicton was laid out in the grand manner and contains unusually fine conservatories and a water garden in the Italian style begun in 1735. Tradition says that it was built following the designs of Le Nôtre, the French landscape architect of Vaux-le-Vicomte and Versailles, but Le Nôtre died in 1700 and there is no definite record that he ever came to England. The Pinetum is world famous for its collection of conifers.

One enters from the car park at the top of the Italian garden and comes first to the fine range of ornamental greenhouses probably built towards the end of the eighteenth century. The centre is open and known as The Temple. It is flanked on each side by what used to be an orangery but is now a café. Three niches on the front of the building hold busts of the Duke of Wellington, Lord Nelson and Sir Walter Raleigh. To the east are the Tropical

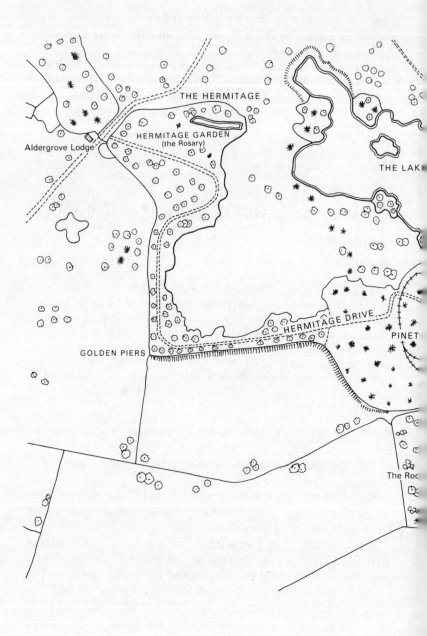

THE HERMITAGE

HERMITAGE GARDEN
(the Rosary)

Aldergrove Lodge

THE LAK

HERMITAGE DRIVE

PINET

GOLDEN PIERS

The Roc

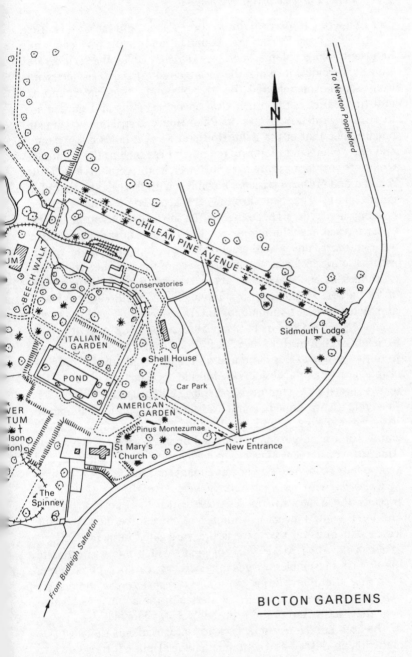

To Newton Poppleford

N

CHILEAN PINE AVENUE

BEECH WALK

UM

Conservatories

ITALIAN GARDEN

POND

Shell House

Car Park

Sidmouth Lodge

AMERICAN GARDEN

Pinus Montezumae

New Entrance

VER TUM (Ison (ion)

St Mary's Church

The Spinney

From Budleigh Salterton

BICTON GARDENS

and Temperate Houses, to the west the Cactus and the Cool House. In the Tropical House are bananas and bougainvilleas and luxuriant foliage plants such as *Maranta* while the Temperate House is colourful with the orange-red *Streptosolen jamesonii* from South America and the ever-blooming *Lantanas*, mimosas and the scarlet bottle-brush *Callistemon speciosus* and gardenias. In a small garden nearby is the Palm House, a striking curvilinear building like that of the Palm House at Kew. It holds a few palms and other plants not requiring too much heat such as the mimosas, which are very large, and a passion flower, leptospermums from New Zealand and *Solanum crispum*, a climber with flowers like that of a potato plant. The beds around are kept bright with summer bedding such as dwarf begonias, scarlet salvia and ageratum. On the upper terrace near the temple is a fine old deodar cedar and there are two more, one at either end of the rectangular pond which with its fountain forms the centre piece of the scheme. The cedar on the left as one looks from above is particularly fine and is one of the largest in the country, having been mentioned by Elwes and Henry in the famous book on *The Trees of Great Britain and Ireland*. Its measurement by Alan Mitchell in 1968 gave it 103 ft in height with a girth of over 18 ft. The ground falls steeply down from the temple to this pond and on the other side rises through a vista of grass to an obelisk on the hillside opposite (erected in 1743) which served as a landmark for ships sailing up the River Otter. The pond is surrounded by fine lead statues on plinths and upright Irish yews. Below it and on the two sides is a supplementary canal. The Italian garden is bounded by brick walls on which the American evergreen *Magnolia grandiflora* has been planted and kept neatly trimmed. Other magnolias on the terrace include *M.campbellii* with its vast pink flowers in early spring and *M. tripetala*, the American umbrella tree which has enormous leaves and large white flowers in summer, tending to be hidden by the leaves. An unusual tree here is the variegated form of *Thujopsis dolabrata* the Hiba Arbor Vitae of Japan which has white tips to the shoots. It resembles a *Thuja* in general appearance. For summer flowering there are large trees of *Eucryphia cordifolia* and *E.x nymansensis*. One of the oldest wisterias in the country is planted near the Cactus House and is probably 150 years old.

The area known as the American Garden adjoins the west side of the Italian Garden and contains the Shell House. It runs down to the road including the new entrance drive and the area by the churchyard. It was intended to plant here trees and shrubs native to America but this has only been partially followed. If one enters from the top of the Italian garden one comes to the Shell House, one of the peculiarities of Bicton. It was built about 1845 and renovated in 1963. Most of the shells are tropical from the Bahamas and the West Indies but there are also some collected on the local beach at Budleigh Salterton. The Shell House is made of flints and in front is a rockery through which water continually flows. There are some fine trees in the American garden among which I noted a strawberry tree, *Arbutus andrachne* from the Mediterranean with fine coloured bark, *Catalpa bignonioides* the Indian bean tree and an exception to the American rule, as is also a davidia, the pocket handkerchief tree from China. For autumn colour there is a fine *Nyssa sylvatica*, the tupelo, and there are massive clumps of azaleas including some of the sweet scented later flowering kinds such as *Rhododendron viscosum*. But the finest tree in the area is the Mexican *Pinus montezumae* in good health, near the church. Its long needles are a silvery-blue in large clusters and it spreads as widely as it is tall. Although a mountain tree from Mount Popacatapetl near Mexico City, it is tender in most areas, but so beautiful that it can claim to be the most beautiful pine in English cultivation but alas is rarely seen. Also notable are some fine *Podocarpus salignus* from Chile, elegant evergreens with long pointed leaves.

To visit the Pinetum go back through the lower end of the Italian garden and through the iron gates on the other side near the bottom of the terrace. The original Pinetum was started in 1840 and so there are many trees of a good age. In fact it contains many of the largest specimens in the country. It has, however, been kept up to date and young trees planted to grow on to take the place of those lost. It covers a large area with winding roads and there is also a model railway which is the easiest way to see it if one does not have much time. Trains leave from a little station by the car park at regular intervals. The narrow gauge railway was built in 1962 and is a mile in length. There is one steam engine named 'Woolwich' and two diesel ones 'Carnegie' and 'Bicton' and three covered passenger coaches and some open ones painted royal blue. The gauge of the track is 18 in. Further details are given in a special booklet on sale at the entrance.

Some of the old specimens are fantastic, for instance *Cryptomeria japonica* was 110 ft tall and among the largest in the country, the Leyland cypresses were 88 ft and 105 ft and probably some of the earliest planted but still only 54 years old. *Juniperus chinensis* was 60 ft and there were thujas well over the 100 ft. *Pinus radiata* at 90 years old had a girth of 22 ft 6 in and was a very venerable and handsome old tree. The *Cupressus macrocarpa* were enormous and probably some of the largest in the country. The Pacific coast American conifers were particularly well represented and there were good trees of *Pinus ponderosa* and *Pinus coulteri*, a younger tree with beautiful bloom on the young shoots and with long needles. *Abies cephalonica* was one of the largest specimens I had ever seen.

More unusual trees we noted included *Podocarpus macrophyllus* of 12 ft, *Podocarpus andinus*, *P.nubigenus* and *P.salignus*, a very large specimen, *Torreya grandis* a rare tree from China, allied to *Cephalotaxus* and somewhat resembling a much broader leaved yew. Some of the trees often suggested as dwarfs for the rock garden controverted that rating, for instance *Chamaecyparis lawsoniana* 'Wisselii' was over 80 ft tall with a girth of 11 ft, distinctive with its glaucous stiff growth and bright red young male cones. Another interesting conifer close to it was *C.lawsoniana* 'Filiformis' in which the terminal branchlets hang down vertically like cords. Others include the Tasmanian cedar *Athrotaxis cupressoides* which was 27 ft when last measured in 1968, and the Bhutan Cypress *C.torulosa* with its hanging branches. There are also very fine specimens of the commoner conifers such as Sitka spruce, Monterey pines, *P.radiata* and Douglas fir. I also noticed a nice young tree of the rarer and rather tender *Pinus lambertiana* well furnished to the ground.

The path through the Pinetum leads to a rustic building called The Hermitage built as a summer house in 1839 by Louisa, Lady Rolls from wood and lined with basket work. A small ornamental lake lies below it. The floor inside is made of deer 'knuckle bones' and the outside is covered with 'fish scale shingles' of wood. Round the Hermitage are collections of rhododendrons and azaleas. The collection of oaks is also extensive, *Quercus phellos*, the willow oak is 50 ft tall, *Q.acuta* is a large tree while *Q.myrsinaefolia*, the bamboo leaved oak also from Japan, is a tree rarely seen. *Zelkova carpinifolia*, an elm-like tree from the Caucasus, is enormous, 84 ft in height with several stems and covered with interesting green flowers.

This used to be known as *Z.crenata*. Those requiring further information on the trees should consult Mr N.D.G. James's booklet *The Trees of Bicton* (Basil Blackwell) which is on sale at the gate. It contains a complete catalogue of the trees and their measurements and shows this as perhaps the best documented collection in the country. I am grateful to him and to Mr Alan Mitchell of the Forestry Commission for his measurements. There is also an avenue of monkey puzzles planted in 1842 out of pots and now ranging from 60–80 ft in height but this leads from the Sidmouth Lodge and is on land belonging to the Devon County Council and not usually shown to the public except on request.

Castle Drogo

The National Trust

One mile W of Drewsteignton in Devon and two miles N-E of Chagford, approached from the A30 Exeter–Oakhampton road and signposted from Crockernwell or from the A382 Bovey Tracey–Moretonhampstead road signposted from Sandy Park. Open daily April–end October 11 am–1 pm and 2–6 pm. House also open. Restaurant. A rhododendron garden overlooking Exmoor and an enclosed garden made by the late Mr Julius Drewe and given to the National Trust in 1975 by Mr Anthony Drewe and Dr Christopher Drewe. Soil acid. Rainfall high.

Castle Drogo is a fortress-like building of granite blocks built in a commanding position overlooking Dartmoor by the late Sir Edwin Lutyens for Mr Julius Drewe between 1911 and 1930. Apart from a small planting of shrubs against the castle the garden lies away from the house to the right of the drive as one enters. No sign of the garden can be seen from the Castle. It is a very exposed position and the main gardens are enclosed with high yew hedges and are terraced. The planting was designed by Mr George Dillistone. The rhododendrons below were planted by Mr Basil Drewe after the 1939–45 war and are on the side of the hill

approached by a grass walk from the Castle. It is surprising how
well they have grown in this exposed position.

On the Castle in various alcoves I noted a fig by the chapel,
Garrya elliptica with its long tassels and *Camellia japonica*, but Mr
Drewe wanted the Castle to stand free of vegetation enjoying the
marvellous view from the terraces by the front door when the
wind permits. The slopes leading from it have been kept wild with
bracken and foxgloves. Leaving the corner of the terrace by a grass
walk, however, down a few steps one comes to Mr Basil Drewe's
shrub garden facing south west. *Rhododendron yunnanense*, a tall
shrubby species with masses of pale lilac pink flowers has grown
well and I also noticed R.'Arthur Osborn' with dark red flowers,
R.aberconwayi with saucer-shaped white flowers and *R.vaseyi* a
deciduous American species with pale pink flowers before the
leaves. R.'Nobleanum', a form from Exbury flowered here in late
October. Magnolias were also growing well and I noticed *Magnolia
dawsoniana*, 20 ft, *Magnolia campbellii* subsp *mollicomata* and also its
deep purple form 'Lanarth'. *Acer capillipes* showed its conspicuous
hanging red seed heads in autumn and *Acer griseum* its fine peeling
mahogany bark. There are also large eucryphias for summer
flowering and *Viburnum davidii* for its fine pleated foliage and
turquoise berries.

The terraced gardens are entered in the corners by four little
quincunxes of lime cut like flat boxes of foliage on bare stems which
have been underplanted with autumn-flowering *Cyclamen neapolitanum*. The main bulk of the lower terrace is planted with roses
with herbaceous borders under the yew hedges. Here I noticed the
Kaffir Lily *Schizostylis coccinea* flowering well in October with
crimson and pink flowers. At the head of the steps are yuccas and
wisterias and above the rose garden are two large *Cotinus coggygria*
(Rhus), attractive in their autumn colour. *Rosa omeiensis*
'Pteracantha' is conspicuous with its translucent crimson thorns
and bordering the walk up to the lawn are azaleas, berberis,
enkianthus, *Viburnum davidii* and a group of large *Eucryphia
glutinosa* with white flowers in August and *Hoheria lyalii* with
clusters of white flowers a little earlier in July. This leads to a large
round lawn enclosed by a trimmed yew hedge and so out again to
the car park.

Castle Hill

The Lady Margaret Fortescue

Near Filleigh. 3½ miles W of South Molton on A361 to Barnstaple. April–October. Gardens open by written appointment with owner for personally conducted tours, preferably parties of 12 or more. House also open. Woodland and formal garden with some very large trees. Soil acid over sandstone. Rainfall high but average for area.

The garden at Castle Hill in North Devon and the woodland behind the house offer a very varied setting for choice plants and this has been taken advantage of. In front of the house is a more formal setting with clipped yews, some rose beds and curving herbaceous borders as well as unusually fine urns and sculptures, all set in a pastoral and wooded countryside.

As one approaches the courtyard behind the house near the entrance arch it is worth pausing to look at unusually fine specimens of a spreading Lucombe oak and also an old cedar. Inside the courtyard a cliff ascends steeply on the north side opposite the back of the house but there are paths up it and it is well worth the effort to ascend since in the upper parts, where the ground spreads out, lilies and rhododendrons have been planted. This has formed a well drained site where some of the lilies have become naturalised. Here such plants as the vast golden striped and spotted *Lilium auratum* and such hybrids as 'Pink Glory' and 'Parkmanni', the cross between *L.auratum* and *L.speciosum*, flaunt their magnificent flowers in July and even August and have settled down well and various orange hybrids have almost naturalised themselves. They grow in groups between rhododendrons such as the large white 'Polar Bear', flowering late in July, and masses of yellow and flame coloured azaleas. *Eucryphia* 'Nymansay' covered with its white flowers in late summer forms a good background between the cliff and the wood. The slopes are covered with cyclamen in autumn and crocuses in spring. In early spring there is mimosa. *Acacia dealbata* flowers near the base of the cliff in one corner while Virginia creeper rambles scarlet over the rocks in autumn. The autumn-flowering *Eupatorium ligustrinum* has made a large shrub

with masses of fluffy white flat heads of flower in September. It is
a plant which deserves to be more widely grown. Blue-grey-leaved
eucalyptus stand out well against the landscape planted near the
top. A gradual path leads round the hill and down through the
dell of the River Bracey to an ornamental stone Palladian temple
with a bog garden in front. *Paeonia lutea ludlowii* the yellow tree
peony has been planted in large groups and are covered with its
cup-shaped flowers raised above the fine leaves unlike those of the
ordinary form. I regard this as one of the best plants introduced
first by Kingdon Ward from South East Tibet and then later by
Ludlow and Sherriff. *Halesia carolina* and *H.monticola vestita* dripping
with white bells in spring have made large bushes and there are
numerous choice camellias, rhododendrons, azaleas and magnolias. This part is primarily a spring garden with some later autumn
colour. The damper parts are carpeted with candelabra primulas
in masses and also the mauve drumsticks of *Primula denticulata*,
which did not seem to have suffered over much from the drought
of 1976 owing to the thick carpets of leaf mould among which
lilies of the valley are spreading. Beside the temple are the silvery
leaved weeping pears, an effective architectural adjunct to the
building, while meconopsis such as the very intense blue saucers of
M.grandis as well as other seedlings, flower well by the stream.
Yellow azaleas provide colour in spring and again in autumn with
their scarlet foliage while the translucent red berries of *Viburnum
betulifolium* give good colour in autumn. The stem of *Acer griseum*
with its peeling mahogany bark stands out. Other plants I noticed
here were the yellow montbretia *Crocosmea* 'Solfatare' as well as
the unusual *Rhododendron glaucophyllum luteiflorum* and groups of
the pale pink *R.williamsianum* hybrids. 'Temple Belle' and 'Bow
Bells' with their drooping bells and fine rounded foliage. Hemerocallis grow along the dell mingling with the ferns and provide
colour in the summer. The garden of choice plants as well as the
lilies of the cliff garden have been largely planted and cared for by
Mr and Mrs Anthony Sampford who live in part of the house. All
this is well worth a visit in spring. I also noted striking shrubs of
Photinia 'Red Robin' with its bright red colour in the young leaves.

Further round the hill the grass is full of daffodils, primroses and
bluebells and some very fine trees are among the long grass. Here is
one of the largest sitka spruces in the country, a wide spreading
tree with its branches down to the ground. When last measured

1 *Magnolia campbellii* in full bloom in early March at Sharpitor, Salcombe.
The chief glory of this interesting garden

2 An unusual hybrid of *Rhododendron Williamsianum* near entrance at The Garden House, Buckland Monachorum, Nr. Tavistock

3 *Erythronium revolutum* in the Woodland Garden of Knightshayes Court, Nr. Tiverton

4 The top of *Magnolia sargentiana robusta* showing an abundance of flower at Caerhays Castle, Cornwall

5 *Eucalyptus ficifolia* at Tresco Abbey, Isle of Scilly

by Alan Mitchell of the Forestry Commission in 1970 it was 138 ft tall and 24 ft 10 in. in girth, the largest girth recorded. It may have been one of the earliest planted soon after its introduction by David Douglas from California in 1831 through the Royal Horticultural Society. There is also a magnificent cut-leaved beech probably about 200 years old drawn up by the side of the hill and the rich moist soil.

As we go back to the front of the house we pass more fine beeches and other outstanding trees. A group of young *Metasequoias* is growing well by the river.

In the front of the house the scene becomes more formal with grass terraces, wide but shallow steps and beautiful ballustrading with only a few beds of colourful flloribunda roses. The urns are massive but very fine while leading down to the lower terrace a pair or recumbent lions in stone flank the steps. Below is a pair of sphinx with a grouping of pillared yews clipped flat on top. On the lowest terrace is a fine cedar and the view leads off across the fields below. To the left at the end of the terrace are a pair of herbaceous borders with roses leading up to the end of the stables with their decorative green domes. Grey-leaved plants such as rue 'Jackman's Blue', sedums and artemisia make contrast in the borders.

Castle Hill is a fine garden, in front a fitting accompaniment of a great house and in the dell and cliff garden an area of choice plants where the potentialities of a favoured site have been developed in an unusual and successful way.

Dartington Hall

Dartington Hall Trustees

S of Buckfastleigh off the A38, follow the A384 for about 5 miles, then follow signpost or NW by same road from Totnes. Garden open daily throughout year in aid of National Gardens Scheme and other charities. Great Hall also open. Soil acid. Rainfall average for area.

DARTINGTON HALL

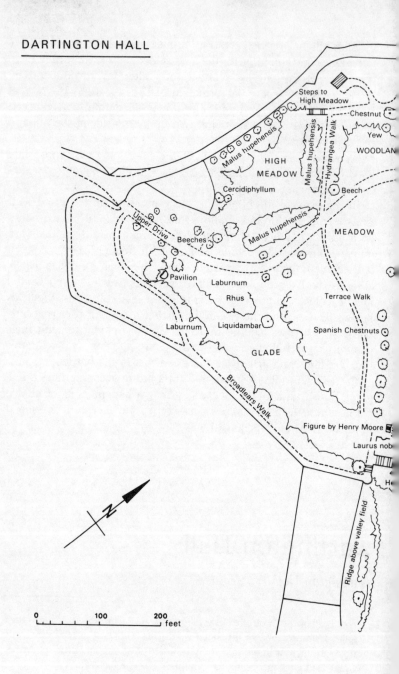

Steps to
High Meadow

Malus hupehensis

Chestnut

Yew

HIGH
MEADOW

Malus hupehensis

Hydrangea Walk

WOODLAN

Cercidiphyllum

Beech

Malus hupehensis

MEADOW

Upper Drive

Beeches

Pavilion

Laburnum

Terrace Walk

Rhus

Liquidambar

Spanish Chestnuts

Laburnum

GLADE

Broadlears Walk

Figure by Henry Moore

Laurus nob

H

Ridge above valley field

N

0   100   200
              feet

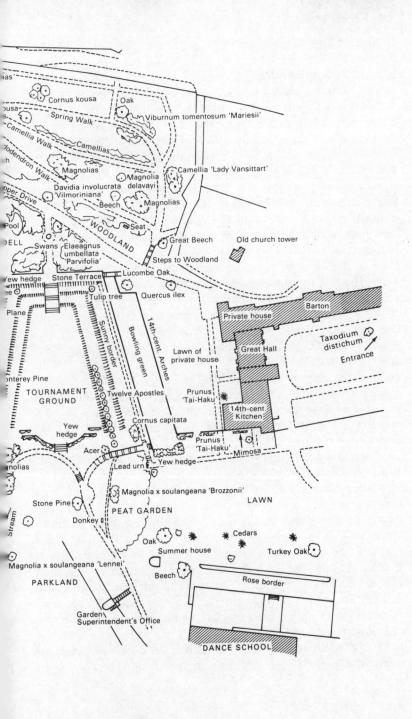

Cornus kousa
Oak
Viburnum tomentosum 'Mariesii'
Spring Walk
Camellia Walk
Camellias
Camellia 'Lady Vansittart'
Magnolias
Magnolia
delavayi
Davidia involucrata
'Vilmoriniana'
Beech
Magnolias
Rhododendron Walk
Seat
Great Beech
Old church tower
Pool
Swans
Elaeagnus
umbellata
'Parvifolia'
DELL
WOODLAND
Steps to Woodland
Yew hedge
Stone Terrace
Lucombe Oak
Tree
Tulip tree
Quercus ilex
Plane
Private house
Barton
Taxodium
distichum
Great Hall
Sunny border
Bowling green
14th-cent. Arches
Lawn of
private house
Entrance
Monterey Pine
TOURNAMENT
GROUND
Twelve Apostles
Prunus
'Tai-Haku'
14th-cent.
Kitchen
Yew
hedge
Cornus capitata
Acer
Prunus 'Tai-Haku'
Mimosa
Lead urn
Yew hedge
Magnolias
Magnolia x soulangeana 'Brozzonii'
LAWN
Stone Pine
Donkey
PEAT GARDEN
Oak
Cedars
Summer house
Turkey Oak
Magnolia x soulangeana 'Lennei'
Beech
Rose border
Stream
PARKLAND
Garden
Superintendent's Office
DANCE SCHOOL

Dartington Hall Gardens are like those of an Oxford or Cambridge College round an old fourteenth century building. Many designers have contributed to them and one comes on a statue by Henry Moore, perfectly placed at the foot of ancient chestnuts, a little statue of a donkey by Willie Soukop, or a pair of granite swans all fitting naturally into the landscape. It is a garden where design predominates but yet it has combined design with plants in an unusual way, the formal blending into the informal. When Dorothy and Leonard Elmhirst bought Dartington there was little here except the lawn and some fine old trees. They have built it up into an active community in which the garden plays a large part. There is nothing else quite like it in the country. It is a garden for all seasons in which there is much to be seen throughout the year, a garden which depends on form and contrast of foliage rather more than on brilliance of colour. It is a restful garden throughout the year. There is a long drive up through fine Devon scenery and then one comes to the entrance into the courtyard, mediaeval like that of a Cambridge college. This has been cleverly planted round the walls with silver and yellow, *Potentilla fruticosa*, *Senecio laxifolius*, hebes and teucrium. Climbers include ceanothus, vitis and rose 'Mermaid', beautiful both in foliage and in flower. On the right of the arch is an enormous *Trachelospermum jasminoides*, a climber with starry white flowers. It is fragrant and in full flower in October. Near the entrance is a fine *Taxodium distichum*, 50 ft tall, lovely with its fresh green foliage. It apparently has its roots down in an old manorial well. It had not coloured by October but later becomes a strong rust before dropping its leaflets. Just outside is a fine *Ginkgo biloba*.

Passing round the end of the great hall to the left one comes on a magnificent plant of the mimosa covering the wall and beautifully trained in winter back to the wall. It faces south east and begins to flower early in January. It is certainly the finest I know in England and must be glorious with its yellow bobbles and grey foliage. It grows right up to the top of the wall and is as much across. In front of it are old prunus 'Tai-Haku', some of the oldest in England. Also against the wall is a very fine *Solanum crispum*, a climber with mauve flowers all through the late summer and early autumn, like those of a potato.

On the south wall of the hall itself is an enormous *Magnolia grandiflora* 'Goliath', the best form for flowering especially when young. This, however, must have been here at least 100 years. Beneath it *Crocus tomasinianus* spreads along the border flowering in February and March. Going down to the lower terrace to the bowling green on each side of the steps are the fine trunks of *Myrtus luma (apiculata)*, a beautiful terracotta-orange brown. They have at least 15 ft of clear stem and are surely the finest trunks that can be grown here. On the old terraces beside the tilt yard are 12 venerable old round clipped Irish yews, clipped horizontally on top and known as the twelve apostles. The closely mown grass banks here are most unusual and fit very well. The old jousting lawn of the tournament green is mediaeval and the sport is some-times revived here. The original builder of Dartington was John Holland, the Duke of Exeter and half-brother of Richard II, and he has been described as a jouster of international fame. This was in the fourteenth century.

On the far side is an unusually fine old *Pinus radiata*, the Monterey pine, 100 years old, and above it seven very old sweet chestnuts with lovely fissured bark, rippling round the trunk. They are thought to be 400 years old. At the end is the *Reclining Lady* statue by Henry Moore looking out over the landscape and placed here by the artist. This brings us to the top of the long steps designed by Percy Cane who also planted many of the rhododendrons and shrubs in the azalea dell. They are planted with white tree heathers, *Erica arborea alpina*, at the top and lower down by magnolias *M x soulangiana* and its form 'Lennei'; they have grown large and are lovely now in May, flowering abundantly. On the hillside across the valley a planting for autumn colour has been made with blocks of *Euonymus alatus*, a lovely shrimp pink, maples, *Acer japonicum* in variety, *Oxydendrum* the sorrel tree from America, flowering and colouring late; *Photinia villosa*. A path leads off to the left to the nursery. In front of the Dance School a group of cedars has been planted and we can return along the sunny herbaceous border planted for summer effect. Pale yellow is the predominating colour, verbascum, hemerocallis, the older pale kinds, *Thalictrum glaucum* with tall blue foliage and yellow flowers, rue and fennel and *Potentilla fruticosa* forms. At one end is an unusually fine *Cornus capitata* at its best with its sulphur yellow bracts in late June and July, at the other a fine tulip tree. *Clematis montana* has been planted to run along the top of the wall. On the terrace above is one of the finest trees at Dartington, a Lucombe oak, *Quercus hispanica* 'Lucombeana'. This was originally raised by Mr Lucombe a nurseryman near Exeter about 1762. This is over 100 ft tall and quite as much across.

This brings us to the beginning of the woodland walks though round the house in autumn we should notice fine beds of *Nerine bowdenii*. A fine *Quercus ilex* stands at the corner. In the magnolia walk there is a fine *M.campbellii* and also a large *M.x veitchii*, its hybrid with *M.denudata*. There are three paths running through the woodland here and leading up to the high meadow. *Magnolia delavayi* with its vast evergreen leaves is doing well and worth pausing at and so are *M.hypoleuca* and *M.sargentiana robusta*, earlier in flower. So is a large *Davidia involucrata*, the pocket handkerchief tree. A number of the tender *Maddenii* rhododendrons such as the sweetly scented 'Lady Alice Fitzwilliam' flower freely in spring and spread their scent. Smaller are *R.williamsianum* and some of its hybrids. *R.*'Loderi King George' rarely fails with its large floppy flowers. The evergreen azaleas, particularly the white 'Palestrina' make a fine effect. The use of ground-cover plants is worth noting and there is hardly any bare earth showing. It also enhances the effect of the shrubs as well as saving much labour. The camellia walk is lovely in spring with varieties of *C.japonica* and *C.x williamsii*, and a few plants of *C.reticulata*. Some of the old japonicas have now reached a good size. In autumn, November *Camellia sasanqua* 'Narumi-gata' starts to flower with attractive scented white flowers tinted with pink. It is one of the few *sasanqua* which seems to flower at all freely in England. The azalea dell at the end of the terraces is ablaze in spring with some of the Exbury hybrids and also the later flowering Ghent azaleas as well as the evergreen kurumes. A few old London planes provide height above them and a little shade. This leads up to the high meadow area with a large planting of *Malus hupehensis* and *Cercidiphyllum japonicum*. The malus is a good tree covered in late spring with white flowers slightly pink tinted in bud. It also bears good crabs in autumn. The *Cercidiphyllum* has lovely soft autumn colour, very variable.

In spring everywhere is covered with spring bulbs, anemones, scillas, dog tooth violets, cyclamen and narcissus, mostly white. In autumn there is a fine flowering of *Cyclamen neapolitanum*. The hydrangeas are fine, mostly 'Blue Wave' and *H.villosa*, more beautiful to me than the large mop-headed ones. Higher up the stewartia give summer flower, effective bark pattern and some autumn colour; *S.pseudocamellia* and *S.koreana* are both grown. In the glade there is a fine colouring specimen of *Liquidambar styraciflua*, magnificent every autumn. *Magnolia* x *watsoni* is late-flowering in June but has the strongest scent of any magnolia. Another unusual plant here is *Staphylaea holocarpa* 'Rosea', most lovely in early spring with its pink flowers. *S.colchica* is also covered with white ones a little later in May. The planting of the woodland glades is designed to give something at all seasons. For early spring there are *Corylopsis*, *C.willmottiae* and *C.spicata*; for early summer *Ceanothus impressus* and later *Viburnum tomentosum* 'Mariesii' and the yellow roses *R.primula* and *R.hugonis*, to be followed by the deep red *Rosa moyesii*, which has wonderful hips later. For late summer there are eucryphias and the sweet pepper *Clethra alnifolia*, *Cornus florida* 'rubra' and *C.nuttallii* and *C.kousa* are fine in mid May and June and for autumn as well as those previously mentioned *Fothergillas*, *Rhus* and *Berberis*. At the edge of the woodland a small pavilion has been built in memory of Dorothy Elmhirst and there is a wonderful view from it. Here one can pause and remember the beauty which Leonard and Dorothy Elmhirst created and also their many helpers and advisers, in particular Beatrix Farrand and Percy Cane, the designers, and the present Superintendent of Gardens Terry Underhill, who keeps it all so well.

Endsleigh

Endsleigh Fishing Syndicate

Near Milton Abbot, Devon. From Tavistock about 8 miles on A384 Tavistock–Launceston road, past Milton Abbot turn left on road signposted Endsleigh Nurseries. Arboretum open daily by arrangement with Manageress, Endsleigh House. House now managed as a hotel. Famous arboretum planted by Duke of Bedford and his successors. Old rhododendrons. Soil acid, in valleys a deep loam with some clay.

Endsleigh is in a magnificent position overlooking the river Tamar and is a particularly favourable site for trees, some of which have grown to a great size. The paths through the arboretum are kept cut but the undergrowth is high and the trees emerge above it. The arboretum was begun about 1810 by the sixth Duke of Bedford for the pleasure of his Duchess Georgiana who was known as 'Georgy' and several of the compartments into which the estate was split are still known as 'Georgy'. They employed Humphry Repton, the landscape architect, who designed the great terraces stretching away from the house. It is now owned by the Endsleigh Fishing syndicate and the house built by James Wyatville is run as a country house hotel.

Let us leave the house by Repton's great terrace running from it to the East, a broad grass walk for the best part of 300 yards to the two compartments of the Georgy Plantation. The river side Repton left bare of any obstacle to the fine view though it is now obscured by a line of very large rhododendrons, but they are lovely in flower in June. The wide slope he planned on the other side rises from above a low retaining wall of stone blocks of which the face is relieved by a series of blind arches. A path lined with wisterias and rambler roses divides the area lengthways, and at the top another parallel path, running between some 20 pairs of Irish yews, gives access at its further end to the Upper Georgy path.

At the end of the terrace is a fascinating grotto decorated with shells and fossils in the style of the famous grotto at Stourhead, and with a small pool of clear water in the middle. This must surely date from the time of Repton and the Duchess Georgy. Repton's Red Book for the property still exists. The grotto has fine views up and down the Tamar and across the wooded slopes on the far side of the river.

More recent, probably under the hundred years old, and standing as a focal point at the end of the terrace, is a very fine cut-leaved lime, *Tilia platyphyllos* 'Laciniata', still in perfect health. Its height is about 35 ft and it is as much across. A wide path leads on beyond the grotto with the areas known as Lower Georgy on its lower river side and that of Upper Georgy above it and stretching as far as the entrance drive. These two areas, particularly the upper one contain a number of very fine trees. Perhaps the star of them all, for me at any rate, is the *Pinus montezumae* in Upper Georgy which can be seen best from the lower path while one can look across at its silvery grey crown from a parallel path higher up through Upper Georgy although no really clear view can be obtained. It was 65 ft when measured in 1957. There are more trees of this spectacular Mexican species in other parts of the arboretum, but probably none as large. The species was introduced in 1839 but it is doubtful whether we now have in this country any trees dating from this time. Near this tree is also a fine one of the grey drooping *Picea smithiana*, one of the most beautiful of the spruces, while close also is *Picea polita* the tiger-tail spruce with its much stiffer, greener and more prickly leaflets. It was 74 ft in height in 1970.

In this area are also two outstanding Douglas firs, *Pseudotsuga menziesii*, with wide branching near the base, showing that for their earlier years at any rate they must have stood clear of other trees and shrubs. Mitchell recorded two of 140 ft in height in 1963, and in girth at 17 ft 2 in. and 16 ft 11 in., not quite the record but near to it. Their crowns stand out above the surrounding trees and they may well date from near the time of its original introduction in 1827. There are also in this area several enormous *Tsuga heterophylla* well over 100 ft, *Thuja plicata* and *Cryptomeria japonica*, one of which is recorded as 'Gracilis', a tree of 80 ft at least. Two cryptomerias at Endsleigh were recorded by Mitchell as 120 ft and 93 ft in 1970. A tall *Cedrus atlantica* 'Glauca' seemed about 120 ft in height and had a girth of 11 ft 6 in. at 4 ft. It had obviously been drawn up by the surrounding vegetation, but still had a good crown. A particularly noteworthy and lovely tree is *Chamaecyparis lawsoniana* 'Pendula', a tall narrow tree with rather glaucous hanging branchlets, estimated at 77 ft. Beside it was a large *Thuja plicata*, slightly taller. A small fastigiate tree about 30 ft tall of a glaucous form of *Juniperus chinensis* still grows near the lower path with its original massive iron label of *Juniperus sheppardii*. Throughout the area are many large spreading bushes of Japanese maples and these must present a magnificent sight in autumn.

In the Lower Georgy area below the main path are some magnificent Corsican pines and a very tall *Sequoia sempervirens*, probably about 125–130 ft in height.

If we return to the house by ascending some steps near the end of the grass terrace by the cut-leaved lime and then turn into the yew walk in the area known as Garden East we pass a fine cut-leaved beech, a very large tree of *Eucalyptus gunnii*, about 65 ft in height, the unusual *Thujopsis dolobrata*, a specimen with many trunks, and three trees of *Styrax obassia*, lovely in June with their white hanging bells. Such large specimens are uncommon. It is distinguished from the more common *S. japonica* by the larger leaves and flowers. Near it was a tall *Eucryphia glutinosa* of about 20 ft.

The years about and just after 1810 were great times for the introduction of new rhododendron hybrids, the kind we now know as 'old hardy hybrids', based on *R. arboreum*, *R. caucasicum* and *R. ponticum* and Endsleigh in early June was bright with these. Few shrubs are capable of making a greater contribution in numbers of flowers and in colour to the scene, especially when they are old and have grown to a great size in a favourable environment. There are none of the more recent hybrids of this half of this century. Most striking among them is 'Sappho' with large trusses of white flowers each with a prominent dark maroon blotch near the base. 'Endsleigh Pink' also originated there and is still one of the finest pinks of this group although unfortunately it is seldom listed now.

The late flowering deciduous azaleas of the Ghent group are also very plentiful and lovely. Some of the older ones raised between 1830 and 1850 such as the white and yellow 'Daviesii', and the orange 'Unique' are still well worth growing and are heavily scented. Early June is undoubtedly the peak period for colour at Endsleigh.

The larger part of the Arboretum occupies land to the north and west of the house and is best approached by a path up a narrow valley, known as the Dell, watered by a small stream. In all of these there is much planting dating from the sixth Duke's successors to the time before the Second World War and the death of the ninth Duke in 1891 and of Herbrandt the eleventh in 1940. His memory is still green and he is revered by the older retainers on the estate and is always referred to as 'Gran'fer Duke', and probably he planted trees in these areas and also particularly the large compartment known as the Dell and Higher Edgecumbe. The older trees may date from the time of the seventh Duke, who rehabilitated the finances of the Bedford Estates after the death of the extravagant sixth Duke, Georgy's husband, and his successors. It may be that the eleventh Duke was a subscriber to the Wilson collections from China since a number of the older trees are among his introductions such as *Abies delavayi* var *fabri*. Alternatively they may have been purchased from the great Veitch nurseries.

We cross the remains of the rock garden, now overgrown, on the left and, before the valley is opened up, the old wall of a large greenhouse on the right. Just beyond a more modern greenhouse is a tall *Camellia reticulata*, which I was told was the double form *flore-pleno*, a rare tree and beside the path a fine weeping Wych Elm, *Ulmus glabra* 'Pendula'. The valley opens out here and one can see well many of the bigger trees in the areas known as Stream East and Stream West. Most striking was a fine specimen of the weeping beech, *Fagus sylvatica* 'Pendula', standing just above the stream, and probably about 70 ft tall, a vast green fountain of healthy growth green to the base. Giant *Sequoiadendron giganteum* also dominate the valley. In 1970 Mitchell recorded one of 165 ft with a girth of 22 ft and another of 152 ft with a girth of 18 ft 8 in., but probably these have both reached their maturity and one was going back. Yellow colour was given in June by a large spreading bush of *Acer negundo* 'Auratum' while later the large Japanese maples and the azaleas should give much autumn colour. An unusual tree in this area was *Kalopanax pictus* of which there were several large specimens. This has large deeply lobed leaves and stout thorns even on the trunk and large branches and clusters of white flowers. A member of the *Araliaceae* it gives a slightly subtropical effect to the woodland though it is quite hardy. The silver firs are well represented with two groups of *Abies delavayi* in the Dell, each about 25–30 ft, a group of two *Abies homolepis*, the Nikko fir from Japan, each about 80 ft, and groups of *A.cilicica*, *A.numidica* and *A.cephalonica* of nearly the same height and of the last species the form 'Appolinis' which has more crowded leaves on the upper part of the shoot and comes from Mt Parnassus in Greece. Most of the trees in the Dell and Higher Edgecombe areas were originally planted in groups of three with reasonable spacing, but where all still survive they are now crowded, especially as no cleaning up of the side branches has been done. In the area known as Higher Edgecumbe there is a specimen of *A.delavayi* of about 50 ft which is an unusual height for this tree in England. In the North Valley East I noted a group of large trees of the glaucous *Abies procera* 'Glauca' of about 65 ft and one of *A.magnifica* of about the same height, while *A.grandis*, a good tree, topped the 100 ft and *A.alba* had reached a similar height. In North Valley East there are two large trees of *A.concolor* of 100 ft.

Among the spruces there are a number of large trees of *Picea abies*, the Norway spruce, which had probably started as grafted plants of garden and dwarf varieties but in which the stock had taken over. There are several trees of *Picea jezoensis* var. *hondoensis*, the unusual Hondo spruce from Japan of 50 ft, and Mitchell recorded in 1963 a tree of 85 ft of this variety but we did not see it. There are several large trees of the Serbian spruce *P.omorika* but they are mostly past their best and do not show well the lovely spire of the best forms. Unusual was a group of four trees of 50 ft of the North American red spruce *P.rubens*, *P.polita*; the tiger tail spruce is well represented in this area and so is *P.orientalis*.

Among the pines there are more trees of *Pinus montezumae*, all notable. One can get a good view of a spreading 40 ft specimen near the pond at the head of the North Valley. Beside it is an old tree of *Pinus armandii* about 50 ft tall and more across but with unusually short needles for this species. Below the waterfall was an old tree of *P.wallichiana*, a handsome tree in any environment. Behind is a young tree with a good pinkish terracota bark of a birch, probably *B.albo-sinensis* var. *septentrionalis* or possibly *B. utilis*. Alders are represented in the damp ground by the stream by several 50 ft trees of *Alnus serrulata*, the smooth alder, which is regarded by Bean as a close relation of *A.rugosa*. It is certainly a fine plant for its broad dark green foliage and probably also for its long catkins in spring.

Many of the other conifers such as *Cunninghamia*, *Podocarpus*, *Fitzroya*, *Taxus* in various forms, *Cephalotaxus*, *Torreya*, *Athrotaxis* and *Thujopsis* are represented by larger specimens than one usually sees.

A visit to Endsleigh if one looks at the trees in detail is like exploring the jungles from which the trees came in China, Mexico, California and other countries, but a good deal can be seen from the paths and the tree lover will find a visit rewarding. We must accept that the fishing, rather than the trees is the prime interest of the Syndicate and it is a large area to keep under control with few staff.

Flete

*The estate of Lord Mildmay now leased to the
Mutual Households Association*

11 miles E of Plymouth. Nr Ermington and S of Ivybridge on A38.
Garden open May to September, Wednesday and Thursday 2.–4 pm.
House not open. A garden remade on the site of an old garden and
maintained by some of the residents of the MHA. Soil acid over clay
and loam. Rainfall average for area.

Flete stands in a beautiful position in the wooded Devon countryside and commands the valley of the Flete leading down to the
estuary only a few miles away. The garden complements well an
old Elizabethan manor house, largely remodelled and castellated
in 1876 by the architect Norman Shaw. It lies around the house at
the end of a long drive and the garden is now beautifully maintained by several of the residents in the house. The large lawns are
well edged and mown and the planting is a good mixture of the
formal and informal, arranged partly for economy of upkeep. The
entrance comes alive early in spring with masses of naturalised
daffodils. A wide border with a gravel walk forms a terrace round
the house and commands beautiful views to the south and west.
On the lawn is a large cedar of Lebanon, a black mulberry and
good specimens of *Pinus radiata*, very well suited to their setting.
Against the wall of the house a fine specimen of *Hydrangea
petiolaris* has spread widely and flowers well, and nearby is a free
flowering form of *Akebia quinata*. Sheltered corners were full in
autumn of great clumps of *Amaryllis belladonna* and *Crinum* x
powellii flowering freely. A double myrtle, a form of the *M.com-
munis*, is another unusual plant. Also unusual is the tender
Lagerstroemia indica, the crape myrtle from China with deep rose
flowers. It is usually regarded as tender but here it has made a large
specimen against a wall. The tender *Abutilon* 'Ashford Red' also
survives outside and produces masses of its dark strawberry-red
bells. So does the tender mimosa *Acacia armata*, the kangaroo
thorn, a prickly domed shrub by a wall, covered with masses of

deep yellow round fluffy heads of flower in spring. This is usually grown as a greenhouse plant. A small rose garden has been reclaimed above and is now gay in summer.

The courtyard on the west side of the house was designed by Norman Shaw. The pattern of the pebbled floor composed of coloured stones should be seen. It is copied from a design of a courtyard at Haddon Hall in Derbyshire and is a perfect example of a former craftsman's work.

Higher up the grass bank are the water gardens designed by Mr Russell Page, the famous garden architect, in 1925 as a small informal cascade with beds for moisture-loving plants on each side. Here in early summer are masses of candelabra primulas, both yellow and pink and for later effect scarlet *Lobelia fulgens*. A small wishing well surrounded by Osmunda ferns is near the top. Some unusual conifers are also placed there. I noted particularly a group of three spires of the dark green *Chamaecyparis lawsoniana* 'Wisselii', lovely in spring when covered with its little red cones. This is usually sold as a dwarf conifer but when planted out attains quite a large size with stout upright branches. There was also a good specimen of the rare *Cryptomeria japonica* 'Spiralis', usually only a slow-growing bush and known as 'Grannies Ringlets' from the twisted spiral effect of the foliage. Here it has grown into a small tree. Autumn effect has also been considered and there is a very large *Liquidambar styraciflua* growing in the grass near the top but with a broken trunk which colours well and some *Eucryphias*, *E.cordifolia* and *E.* 'Nymansay' flower in late summer. *Magnolia grandiflora* is here a free standing bush with colchicums below, and in the beds are also some good lilies, spikes of the great spotted Japanese *Lilium auratum* and the orange *L.henryi* from China, one of the most vigorous species. The swamp cypress *Taxodium distichum* makes another pillar of fresh green in spring and summer and russet brown in autumn and is a striking feature near the top of the cascade. *Magnolia delavayi* with its huge leathery leaves and white flowers in summer hidden between them and a good large *Magnolia* x *soulangiana* 'Lennei' with its upright rounded globlets of purple are other features near the top of the water garden. In the grass of the lawn are some fine oriental planes, some of the finest of all garden trees with their peeling bark and large palmate leaves. Nearby is a large paved garden in Italian style with stone seats and vases designed by the late Lady Mildmay. Replanting is being carried out to get it back to its one-time splendour.

Moving back towards the house one should not miss a good shrub border in front of the wall of the old kitchen garden. There are some striking and also tender plants on the wall at the back such as *Feijoa sellowiana* with its rounded grey leathery leaves. It flowers freely with its mass of long crimson stamens and sometimes also fruits after a hot summer. I also noted a fine *Campsis*, probably *C.chinensis* which produces large orange red trumpets after a warm summer. There was also a big 'Mermaid' rose with its lovely single yellow flowers and shiny, almost evergreen foliage. A large *Actinidia kolomikta* on the wall shows its remarkable tricoloured variegation of the leaf with white and pink colouring in the part nearer the tip. *Lardizabala biternata* an evergreen climber with decorative glossy leaves and winter flowers of chocolate purple and white and, rarely, purple fruits. In front bushes of the late flowering *Eupatorium ligustrinum* were covered with whitish feathery clusters and further round the border were good specimens of embothrium, the Chilean fire bush, the evergreen *Crinodendron hookeranum*, 30 ft high and hung in spring with deep red little lanterns, introduced by William Lobb from Chile in 1848. Lobb was a Cornishman collecting for Veitch of Exeter. There was also *Drimys winteri* growing freely. It is another South American tree. The little thatched house nearby, once the family's children's playhouse, is now used as a tool shed and its garden used for growing cut flowers for the house: still very pleasant to see and an agreeable reminder of an earlier generation.

A vast old *Cupressus macrocarpa* stands on the lawn and the base of another, now felled, shows the size they had reached. Nearer to the wall is a striking variegated *Aralia*. Contrasting with the cypresses are grey and silver-leaved eucalyptus *E.niphophila*, the Australian snow gum, one of the hardiest, *E.nitens* with long drooping leaves and the unusual *E.glaucescens*.

Finally, in a sheltered position, one should pause at a Grapefruit tree outside, now 8 ft tall. It is very unusual to see one growing outside through the winter in England. Near the entrance are some fine specimens of the silver lime, *Tilia tomentosa*, a tree which is helping us to replace the elms, while in the open woodland below the drive are various rhododendrons which are worth a visit in spring and early summer.

Flete is a garden of considerable variety, soundly designed

originally around an imposing and massive house. Its recovery from the jungle of wartime now owes much doubtless to the good advice and help of Mr John Newell, VMH, the garden adviser to the Mutual Household Association, and to the devoted energies and skills of some of the present inhabitants of the house, which is now divided into numerous separate flats for elderly people.

The Garden House, Buckland Monachorum

L.S. Fortescue Esq

5 miles S of Tavistock. From Tavistock to Plymouth by A386 after about 5 miles turn right to Buckland Monachorum. The Garden House is on right just before Buckland Monachorum. Garden open mid-April—beginning of September, Wednesday 3–7 pm or by previous arrangement in aid of National Gardens Scheme. Plants for sale by arrangement. House not open. A medium sized garden made by present owner and full of choice plants. Soil acid in top part around house, lime in lower old kitchen garden. Shillet. Rainfall high, 50 in.

The Garden House has a medium-sized garden made within the last thirty years but it is packed with carefully selected plants. Only the finest forms of each plant are allowed to remain. Most shrubs are trimmed rigorously and flower abundantly. I have not seen more colour in any garden. Exposed and lying on the south side of Dartmoor it is protected by very tall hedges of x *Cupressocyparis leylandii*, grown to a height of 30 ft and this provides good shelter. The garden is on a hillside facing north and a number of terraces have been built behind the house, sloping down to an old tower and a walled garden.

One enters the garden by a mass of camellias among which 'Donation' is preeminent and laden with flower in early spring. In front are dwarf rhododendrons, hybrids of *R.williamsianum* in various colours and *R.saluenense*, among which a particularly deep-coloured one stands out. *Cyclamen neapolitanum* carpets the ground with pink and white in late summer and makes a fine spectacle. The Garden House has a garden for all seasons and is certainly worth more than one visit throughout the year. Beside the upper drive and by the front door are good forms of *Hibiscus sino-syriacus* flowering in September and free standing away from a wall. The flowers are white or pale pink and with a deep blotch at the base and larger than those of *H.syriacus*. Then by an avenue of cherries the drive divides, the upper drive leads to the house and the lower one to the garden which one enters by a gate in the wall at the bottom and works one's way upwards. The two lower gardens contain largely herbaceous plants and are walled in old stone. I remember particularly a graceful form of hemerocallis with small deep yellow flowers. The larger flowered ones have been largely discarded. Beside it was a deep maroon coloured *Cosmos atrosanguineus* which is perennial, but rather tender; a thick hedge of *Cotoneaster lacteus* up to 6 ft is caressed with clusters of red berries in September but the roots are stopped from spreading by polythene. The old stone tower is a feature of this part of the garden and one can ascend to get a good viewpoint of the ascending terraces. A row of *Picea glauca albertiana conica* makes an unusual feature, green pyramids about 4–5 ft high. Other plants I noticed in September by this lower garden were *Colutea arborescens* with its conspicuous bladder-like seed pods, *Malva moschata*, the white form, and both purple and white forms of *Thalictum dipterocarpum*, which Mr Fortescue told me had withstood the drought well. Sedum 'Vera Jameson' was a semi-prostrate form with pale purple flowers and was also effective. The blue herbaceous clematis *C.heracleifolia* 'Wyevale' was lovely in late August and September growing among other plants. *Abutilon vitifolium* 'Veronica Tennant' and its form 'Tennant's White' do well here and are covered with flower. *Genista cinerea* and *Viburnum* x *chenaultii* and a very good form of dark leaved *Phormium tenax* are notable here. Mr Fortescue considers *V.* x *chenaultii* as the best of the *burkwoodii* cross. I also noted a fine form of *Hoheria glabrata* flowering much later. *Eleagnus* x *ebbingei* makes a good hedging plant here with its silvery foliage. As one ascends the terraces a sloping path leads to a bed of special rhododendrons sheltered by one of the high *leylandii*

THE GARDEN HOUSE

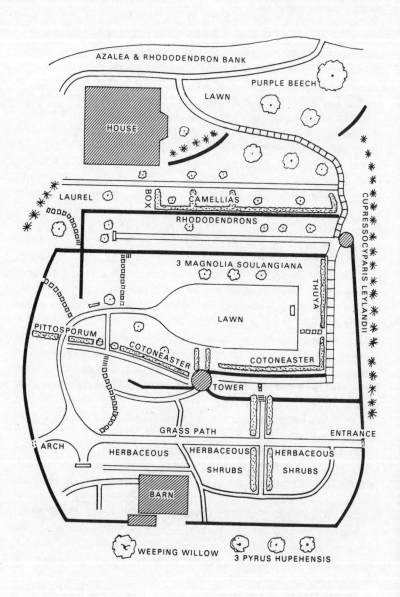

hedges. *R.*'Katherine Fortescue' derived from 'Exbury Hawk' crossed with *R.griffithianum* is one of the finest yellows that I have ever seen, fittingly named after Mrs Fortescue. A tall growing plant with a compact truss. 'Lionel Fortescue' is derived from *R.wardii* 'Ellestee' x 'Windsor Hawk' and promises to be another good yellow. Both were raised at The Garden House. I noticed here also *R.*'Caerhays Philip' derived from *R.concatenans* x *R.cinnabarinum* and one of the best deep yellows.

On the other side of the hedge in a triangular area between the two hedges. *Erica* x *veitchii* flowers freely and contrasts with rhododendron 'Elizabeth', that bright scarlet hybrid of *R.forrestii repens* and *R.griersonianum* and the two flower together. I noticed here also a very good form of the dwarf *R.crebreflorum*, pale shell pink and covered with flower, also a pink Fortescue cross from the same parentage as the famous 'Penjerrick' (*campylocarpum elatum* x *griffithianum*). *Leptospermum scoparium* had grown enormous in this sheltered position. Rhododendron 'Jack Skelton' raised at Trewithen had made a good cream coloured plant near the junction of the drive while *R.arboreum* 'Sir Charles Lemon' displayed well the rusty rufous underneath of its foliage. *Rhododendron* 'Queen Elizabeth II' raised in the Great Park at Windsor was another very fine yellow. The Garden House has more of the best yellows than any other garden I know.

Along the side of the house is a fine wisteria and under it a bed of tender bulbs with a narrow border of more *R.crebreflorum* and other dwarf rhododendrons run along the other side. This leads round the house to the terraces but in spring one should pause for *Clematis indivisa* from New Zealand; usually considered tender and a plant for the cool greenhouse, here it has grown in a protected nook in the wall and gives a mass of flowers, each about $2\frac{1}{2}$ in. across. I have never seen it growing better or flowering so freely. Plants of both the pink and the white lapagerias festoon the old ironwork and glass shelter beside the house and here they flower unusually well. This leads one to the upper terrace where *Camellia japonica* have been grown into a hedge. The single red 'Sylva' is considered by Mr Fortescue to be one of the best. About 10 ft high these are pruned immediately after flowering each year. On the other side against the house tender *Maddenii* rhododendrons are grown and are given protection in winter against the north side of the house, and this has proved successful. On the terrace below is one of the finest *Magnolia salicifolia* that I have ever seen, a pillar of creamy white about 30 ft in height. This is not really a magnolia garden because of its exposure to wind, but this one has certainly proved its possibilities. On the upper terrace *Rhododendron* 'Russautinii' has proved one of the deepest mauves in flower and a very striking plant against the magnolia below. Others I noted here are 'Marcia', a good yellow, 'Tally Ho', bright scarlet as its name implies and later 'Romany Chal', also a deep red. The eucryphias are also good, *E.lucida* x *E.cordifolia* is not one often seen but it does well here and was in full flower in early September. Curiously *E.*'Nymansay' seems to do better on the acid soil of the upper terraces but took longer to come into flower than on the limey soil of the lower gardens. Further down the terraces tree paeonies do well, particularly the dark red *P. delavayi*. Another plant I noted was *Acer pennsylvanicum erythrocladum* with its bright scarlet stems all the winter. In front of the house in a very sheltered position almost coming into the window the finest plant I have seen of *Camellia japonica* 'Alba Plena' grows trained on the wall, its waxy white double flowers are almost perfect. In front of the house *R.* 'Lady Chamberlain', 'Lady Rosebery' and 'Lady Berry' are literally weighed down with flower. Underneath pink *Erythronium revolutum* and 'White Beauty' have been naturalised with forms of *Fritillaria meleagris* flowering freely in the grass, a sight to remember.

This account only mentions a small proportion of the many choice plants in the garden. They are pruned hard, fed well, many with old rotted cow manure, ruthlessly eradicated if they do not do well, but the results are certainly something to remember. It is an example of what a plantsman, who will tolerate only the best, can achieve in a limited time.

Killerton

The National Trust

8 miles N of Exeter by A38 and then B3185 to Broadclyst. Signposted. Open daily throughout year. House now open. A large woodland garden made by the Acland family, specialising in rhododendrons, camellias and magnolias. Given to the National Trust in 1944 by Sir Richard Acland, Bt. Soil acid, volcanic, lying over a basalt outcrop and well drained. Rainfall average for area.

Killerton is an old garden laid out about 150 years ago from parkland and planted by Sir Thomas Acland, Bt, after the Napoleonic wars with the help of Mr Robert Veitch, the founder of the Exeter branch of the famous Veitch nursery. There is still a giant *Sequoiadendron giganteum* which was probably raised from the original seed from California about 1853 and the largest tree is now about 116 ft high. Later many Himalayan and Japanese trees were planted and many rhododendrons grown from Kingdon Ward's seed from his various expeditions, some of which have now reached a great size.

The garden is on a hillside and the paths follow roughly its contours so that one need not climb steeply, while one gets frequent glimpses through the glades down to a wide panorama of fields and low hills towards Dartmoor with rhododendrons in the foreground.

Killerton is primarily a spring garden but there is something to see at all seasons and recent planting for the summer season below the house and beyond it of herbaceous and silver-leaved plants helps to extend the interest. One enters by a gate above the house and the path soon leads to an area of magnolias, dominated when the spring is relatively frost free by a large tree of *M.campbellii*, a good pink form, flowering always long before there is any green on the beeches around. It is at least 40 to 50 ft high now and has a good crown so that it is very magnificent when in flower, often in March. In front is a large tree of the white *M.kobus* which was flowering freely at mid-April. In other parts of the garden there are seedlings from this magnolia, flowering at about 6 ft tall and some with more petals than the parent. Some may have been natural hybrids with *M.stellata*. On the lawn just above the house is a fine Yulan *M.denudata*. It is good to see that young trees of *M.campbellii* and *M.dawsoniana* have been planted for the future.

On the left of the lawn a young *Magnolia cylindrica* has been planted and flowers well. A large *Magnolia stellata* makes a great splash of white early in the season and is very fine; possibly it is the other parent of the very fine *kobus* hybrids already mentioned. Everywhere there are masses of primroses in the bank and there are good groups of camellias; the pale blush 'Salutation' was 10 ft tall and beautiful, and 'Donation', the best of the *williamsii* hybrids about as tall. There are also very large specimens of the North American *M.fraseri* and *M.macrophylla* which flower with the enormous leaves, the tree of *M.fraseri* being about 65 ft high and possibly the largest in the country. It can be recognized by the pale yellow flowers and the auricles at the base of the leaves. The plant of *M.x veitchii*, although not so large as those at Caerhays in Cornwall, may well have been one of the original trees from Veitch. On the lawn near by are some specimens of tulip trees. Very near the house was one reputed to have been the sixth largest in Britain until it was recently felled because of the risk of falling branches; further out on the lawn another, planted in the late 1920s, had grown to a splendid tree of 56 ft by 1964, but is far exceeded by two in the Chapel area nearer the main gate, one of 106 ft, the other of 98 ft. These are by far the largest I have seen. For these measurements as well as others throughout the article I am indebted to Mr Alan Mitchell whose measurements were made for Sir Richard in 1964 so that the present size may often exceed those given here: a few measurements were made since 1964. For summer flower there is a large *M.sieboldii* in front of the magnolia group. On the lawn close up is also a fine *Cornus nuttallii* in full flower in April and underplanted with *Cyclamen repandum*, which was flowering in patches in the grass at the same time. It is a lovely combination. The cornus was planted in 1930 and is now a large spreading tree. Everywhere there are masses of daffodils in the grass, which make a lovely effect in April.

A wide expanse of lawn stretches beyond the house and below the woodland interspersed with large curved beds of old rhododendrons and other trees. The rhododendrons are old hybrids of *R.arboreum*, difficult to name now but the masses are enormous and the colour mostly a good deep red so that the effect in flower is most spectacular. When grown in full exposure like this such rhododendrons form a great solid compact mass and the flower is equally solid. Here they are perhaps 25 ft high and twice as much across.

A good avenue of beeches nearly 100 ft tall leads upwards and underneath them are *Cyclamen repandum* which is one of the spring features of the garden. I have seldom seen them doing better, except perhaps in their native Corsica.

Ginkgo biloba looked well with its fresh green in front of a group of darker foliaged cypresses and must have been lovely in the autumn. This season is also well cared for by large Japanese maples, planted against dark backgrounds and very fine in October.

Eucalyptus, although comparatively young in many cases, are also a good feature and a collection of these will increase in beauty each year. Already *E.gigantea* is 25 ft high and has lovely large drooping glaucous waxy leaves. The value of the decorative bark is also well shown by a large tree of *Stewartia pseudocamellia*. The trunk has a delightful mottled effect of olive green mingled with a warm rusty colouring in irregular patches which shows up from quite a distance. This is surely a tree which deserves wider planting since it flowers also in late summer when shrubs in flower are not so abundant and in autumn its leaves give good yellow and red colouring. In Japan it is reported to reach 50 ft in height and the tree at Killerton must now almost equal that, since in 1964 Mr Mitchell recorded 45 ft for it. Certainly its trunk rivals those of most of the eucalyptus.

Flowering cherries are abundant near the edge of the lawn and look well with daffodils in flower below. On the lawn also is a fine *Davidia involucrata* with several stems, about 30 ft high.

Birches, oaks and *Nothofagus* are quite well represented in the woods as well as the rhododendrons and conifers so that no genus really overpowers the rest. This is a pleasant feature. Mr Mitchell recorded *Quercus borealis* of 90 ft, *Q.canariensis* (*mirbeckii*) of 40 ft, *Q.ilex* of 80 ft with a girth of 17 ft by the house and 75 ft × 13 ft 7 in. by the chapel. *Q.laevigata* is 35 ft and the famous cork oak *Q.suber* 45 ft. The cork of the bark is thick and well developed and makes a very interesting feature. The cork oak is generally regarded as tender, but I have seen quite good specimens in a west Sussex garden also, so perhaps it should be tried more often. *Nothofagus* is represented by *N.obliqua*, a good tree that was 42 ft in 1964 and now looks appreciably larger. Eucryphias also help to make good summer flowering and there is a fine specimen of *E.cordifolia* planted in 1956 and now at least 30 ft tall. Another famous tree is *Styrax obassia* with several stems from the base and about 25 ft in height.

But interesting and beautiful as all these are it was the rhododendrons and unusual conifers which made the greatest effect on me. The rhododendrons all seemed very well grown with sufficient space around each so that most are green right down to the ground with good live branching instead of the tall gaunt specimens one sometimes sees when they have not been thinned in time. *R. arboreum* in its various forms has grown particularly well. I have seen taller specimens in Cornish gardens, but few so well shaped. The white-flowered form of the subsp. *cinnamomeum* was particularly fine, at least 15 ft high and as much across. The flowers are dead white with only a slight purple blotch near the base and the truss is unusually high and full while the underneath of the leaf is as rusty fulvous as any rhododendron. A large tree of *R.arboreum* forma *roseum* there also gave me much pleasure, a rather pale pink form with well-shaped solid trusses of flower, free of any speckling inside. There is also a pale pink flowered *cinnamomeum* and subsp *campbelliae*, a good clear pink form with leaves very rusty below, so that these plants are a notable feature throughout the year. I noted also an unusually fine *campanulatum* with good flower colour and truss, and a fine deep scarlet *R.delavayi*. The larger-leaved species are not abundant, perhaps there is slightly too much wind and exposure for them, but there was a large *arizelum*, though I did not see it in flower. The form of *R.fulvum* had a nice lilac flower with a conspicuous blotch as well as good coloured indumentum. *R.hodgsonii* and *R.coriaceum* were also noted, the latter a form with a very dark blotch but with rather small leaves. *R.praestans* here was pink; notable also was a fine group of *R.venator* (with its pillar box scarlet flowers) 8 ft × 20 ft, placed in front of a vast group of the white 'Dr Stocker' which I placed at 24 yards across. The groups of *R.rubiginosum* and *R. yunnanense* are fine and give lightness to the heavier plantings. They are valuable for this as well as for their abundant flowering. I noted a very fine *R.ciliatum*, also a compact bush about 4 ft × 5 ft across covered with pink flowers, which seemed to me larger and with a fuller truss than in most other forms I had seen. Another in which Sir Richard is particularly interested was *R.polylepis* so covered with purplish-pink flowers that no foliage showed. Some knowledgeable gardeners have said that the somewhat fastigiate form of the Killerton specimen is possibly exceptional in Britain. *R.eclecteum* attracted my attention since it is a species one seldom sees flowering well. Another lovely species was *R.johnstoneanum*, whose creamy white flowers covered the bushes in several forms. This is too tender for colder gardens. For later spring flowering various azaleas of the Ghent group have been planted. The row towards the top of the woodland of the bright orange 'Gloria Mundi' is particularly striking and the bushes are certainly large. But this is only a small selection from the rhododendrons.

The rhododendrons are rivalled only by the conifers in number and quality. There were some rare specimens – *Taiwania crypto-merioides (formosa)* had made a slender and graceful spire 40 ft tall; this may be one of the largest in the country. In habit *Taiwania* has some resemblance to *Cryptomeria* and it is not generally regarded as very hardy but at Killerton it has grown unusually well. The Umbrella pine from Japan, *Sciadopitys verticillata*, had been measured as 41 ft with a girth of 4 ft 10 in., a very unusual size for this rather slow-growing tree and this is one of the finest specimens I have seen. Other rare and tender conifers include *Saxegothaea conspicua*, Prince Albert's yew from Chile and Patagonia, rather like a podocarpus in foliage, *Fitzroya cupressoides* also from Chile which is probably the tallest in Britain, (61 ft in 1970), and *Athrotaxis selaginoides*, the King William pine from the mountains of Tasmania which was recorded in 1962 as 36 ft tall and is now 44 ft with a girth of 1 ft 8 in. The larger of two *Cupressus funebris*, a very rare tree, is 41 ft tall. There is a good *Picea brewerana* with its weeping branchlets near a very ancient chestnut, a combination which I found pleasing. One of the finest specimens is a *Chamaecyparis pisifera* 'Filifera' which also has long weeping branchlets, almost cord-like. There are many more which will repay a visit.

The curving rides through the rhododendrons and other trees lead us down again towards the end of the big lawn past an unusual summer house known as the Bear's hut built about 1840 or 1850 in Victorian rustic style. At the foot of the lawn a summer garden has been made with terraced beds to provide some summer interest for the many holiday visitors who come then. It is planted with herbaceous plants and dwarf shrubs and those with decorative or silver foliage such as bergenias, dwarf yuccas, lavender, santolinas and large masses of helianthemums. In the spring the lateral lines of these make an intrusion across the straight flow of the view down the hill over the surrounding country, but it must be considered for its summer value when there is comparatively little flower on the hill and it does not seem to intrude on the landscape view.

The house itself is not open to the public but on the walls can be seen some interesting and tender plants growing right up to the eaves, in particular on the south-west wall a very fine mimosa, *Acacia dealbata*, which was in full flower in April and very conspicuous, while on the other side nearer the entrance, later in May, the yellow *Sophora microphylla* and *Azara microphylla*, with its chocolate scent and little fluffy heads of deep yellow flowers, were exciting for the connoisseur of plants. Both grow up to the eaves of the house.

Knightshayes Court

Lady Amory and the National Trust

2 miles N of Tiverton; turn right at signpost from A396 Tiverton–Bampton at Bolham. Bequeathed to the National Trust in 1973 by Sir John Heathcot-Amory, Bt. Garden open April–end October daily except Friday and Saturday. 2–6 pm. Choice plants for sale by exit. House also open, of Victorian interest but with collection of very choice pictures. Garden largely a woodland and shrub garden made since 1945 by Sir John and Lady Heathcoat-Amory. Soil sandy loam and shillet over red clay, in woodland acid with pH 4.8, below house neutral. Average rainfall 36 in.

Knightshayes is one of the few large gardens made since the war and undoubtedly one of the most interesting and beautiful. Sir John and Lady Amory combined an unusual degree of artistic taste with a love and knowledge of individual plants and it is this which has made the garden unique. The woodland garden, still being developed, is perhaps their greatest achievement and it compares with the Savill Garden in Windsor Great Park or the old wild garden at Wisley. Sir Eric Savill, a friend of Sir John and Lady Amory, has helped and advised on plantings. A visit in the spring between March and June is probably the most rewarding, but there is plenty of interest to see at all seasons, since it is a well-balanced garden with all manner of plants rather than a collection of one or two genera.

One enters near the Conservatory at the west end of the house and can then walk along the terrace in front of the house, seeing on the right the magnificent views southwards over the valley towards Tiverton. The garden below is dominated by a fine old cedar of Lebanon and has beds largely of shrub roses. There is a group of three fine *Malus hupehensis* on the lawn which gives masses of apple-like flowers in May, pale pink in bud then opening to white; it also gives good autumn colour and reddish yellow fruits.

In the Conservatory opening off the drawing room of the house are early-flowering scented tender rhododendrons of the *Maddenii* series, also some tender abutilons which flower constantly throughout the year. Against the house wall are Banksian roses and blue ceanothus. Under the walls in autumn the brilliant scarlet *Zauschneria californica* and *Z.cana* from Mexico flower freely together with the pink and deeper red forms of the Kaffir lily *Schizostylis coccinea* 'Major' contrasting with the silvery grey foliage of the shrubby and tender *Melianthus major*, surely one of the most beautiful of all foliage plants; in tubs are purple-leaved *Cordylines*. One of the great lessons of this garden is the careful and often striking contrasts of form and colour in the foliage as well as in the flower. On the wall is a very fine *Chaenomeles* 'Rowallane' covered with deep red flowers in April while the unusual *Tulipa saxatilis* from Crete has pale rosy lilac flowers at the foot of the wall at the same time.

Towards the end of the main house is an interesting bed on the left with yuccas for late summer flowering, dimorphothecas, schizostylis, callistemon, and other unusual plants. On the grass banks beyond are several *Corylopsis* and a good eucalyptus which bring you to two unusual raised gardens on the left framed in

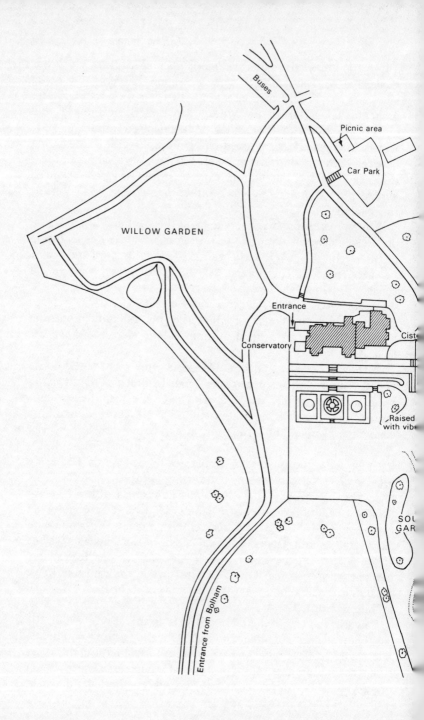

KNIGHTSHAYES COURT

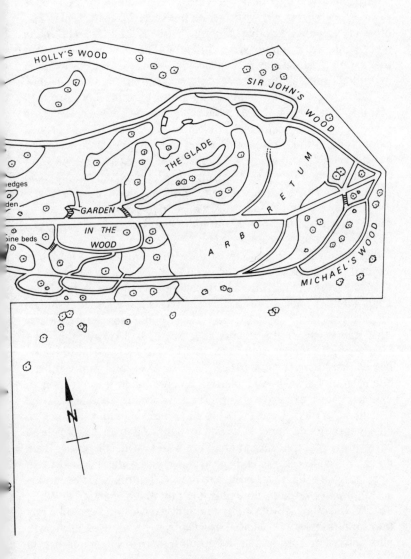

HOLLY'S WOOD

SIR JOHN'S WOOD

THE GLADE

ARBORETUM

edges

den

GARDEN

IN THE
WOOD

bine beds

MICHAEL'S WOOD

N

castellated clipped yew hedges; the first dominated by four well shaped standards, the front two of *Viburnum* x *juddii*, a very fine hybrid raised in 1920, flowering in April and behind two wisterias. At the end stands an old lead cistern dated 1727. In summer it is filled with tender grey-leaved plants. The paths are made of stone with pebbles arranged in a decorative design while the beds have raised stone edges over which flow the silver-leaved creepers and prostrate plants. Notable among these is the *Leucanthemum hosmariense* with white chrysanthemum-like flowers throughout the spring and summer, contrasting with the pink spreading geraniums such as 'Ballerina' and *G.sanguineum* var. *lancastriense*.

The next garden, the old bowling green, is a model of restrained planting just a large round pond with a stone edging, a weeping silver pear, *Pyrus salicifolia pendula* at the side. This is pruned carefully from the centre twice a year to keep an open form taking out all branches that cross others. There is an exceptional and charming statue in a recess and on the sides a few more *Phormium tenax*, the New Zealand flax with their decorative sword-like leaves. This garden, so simple and yet so skilled in its planting, gives me as much pleasure as any part of this marvellously rich garden and is a great contrast to the teeming planting elsewhere. The yew hedges are broadly castellated while by the entrance there are a topiary fox and hounds in full chase along the top.

Below both these beds are two long raised beds with choice alpines and small shrubs. They are surfaced with fine shingle against which the gentians and dwarf bulbs look well. In early April there was a fine *Romulea bulbocodium*, like a small deep mauve crocus coming up in groups. There are silver-leaved plants like *Euryops acraeus* and *Helichrysum retortum* and many others. Some of the silver-leaved plants are given a little protection in winter against excessive damp. Then we mount the steps to the woodland garden. Here the trees have been carefully thinned to allow open glades and to bring in light. All trunks have been cleaned up by a tree surgeon and are kept so. One can either walk down the wide central path or wander along the side paths. In April and May the dwarf bulbs are most delightful. Selected strains of *Erythronium revolutum* the pink dog's tooth violet and of *E.*'White Beauty' have grown unusually tall and vigorous and spread freely into large masses. *Cyclamen repandum* has naturalised itself with pink flowers in April and in the autumn there are again carpets of cyclamen in flower. Wild anemones of many kinds abound. The garden is well labelled and so it is unnecessary or indeed impossible in the space to mention all the exciting plants.

The peat wall garden is lovely in spring with primulas and little ferns between the blocks of peat and behind are the Lenten roses, *Helleborus orientalis*, again carefully selected for the darkest forms and for those which show their flowers rather than hanging them to face downwards. There are good celmisias with their silvery sword-like leaves and large white daisies in late summer. Among the rhododendrons in this area to the south of the main walk are some unusually fine *R.johnstoneanum* with cup-shaped or saucer-shaped creamy scented flowers in May. Rather earlier in April it is worth looking for an unusually dark pink form of *R.moupinense* and also in the main walk a low dome of *R.chamaethomsonii* with scarlet waxy bells. This is an unusually free-flowering form and measured $7\frac{1}{2}$ ft across by $3\frac{1}{2}$ ft high.

Magnolias and camellias abound and flower freely in late March and April while *M.sinensis* and *M.wilsonii* flower in May with large pendulous white flowers among the foliage. Other shrubs to look out for include a large branching specimen of the silver-variegated *Aralia elata*, the red-twigged *Acer* 'Senkaki' and the peeling-barked *Acer griseum*, *Koelreuteria paniculata*, with yellow flowers in August, *Hydrangea aspera*, *Stachyurus praecox* with creamy little bells hanging like lilies of the valley all along the branches in early April, well placed next to the very dark maroon-leaved form of *Pittosporum tenuifolium*. The pink camellia 'Donation' has made a tall bush 15 ft high in as many years and is certainly one of the most floriferous of all varieties. Close by is a big patch of the blue Chatham Island forget-me-not *Myosotidium hortensia*. This grows in the Pacific by the shore and thrives best when top dressed with sea weed or bits of fish. It is well worth the trouble and a real horticultural triumph. The main path leads on into the glade and then on the north side and east end are the more newly planted areas Holly's Wood, Sir John's Wood and last is Michael's Wood named after the head gardener Michael Hickson, so that the whole planted area is now about 25 acres. Below is a newly planted arboretum. Sir John's Wood has been underplanted with primulas and dwarf bulbs. The primulas include masses of *P. gracilipes* with purplish pink flowers in April; also chionodoxas; forms of the wood anemone; *Scilla messanensis*, one of the best spreaders; and the giant celandine also a spreader but very lovely in the spring with its shining rich yellow flowers. Later there are white martagon lilies and willow gentians. Among the trees and shrubs are some rare maples such as *Acer hookeri*, the conspicuous weeping conifer *Dacrydium franklinii*, *Pinus patula* with its long needles of the freshest yellowish green and *Weinmannia trichosperma* from Chile with large pinnate leaves. Also of interest here are various forms of *Photinia* with brilliant red young foliage in spring retained for much of the summer. These are now becoming popular plants and are rewarding for this character. Lady Amory told me that her favourites were 'Red Robin' and 'Robusta', both forms of the hybrid *P.* x *fraseri*. In Michael's Wood there is a large area of prostrate forms of ceanothus and large-leaved rhododendrons, mostly young plants which are only just beginning to flower.

On the way back there is a charming summer house, put up in 1972 to mark the completion of the planting of the glade. A notable feature in the plant on the south side of Philadelphia Lodge is a collection of decorative grasses, probably at their best in late summer and visitors will be surprised at their variation. After descending the steps at the end of the garden in the wood it is worth in summer turning left, by a superb decorated stone seat and a fine specimen of the drooping *Cupressus recurva coxii* below the terrace. Down the hill are collections of shrub roses and further on some later-flowering rhododendrons in great variety and other trees with decorative foliage. In the grass and indeed over much of the garden are masses of daffodils. These have been mostly planted in large groups of a single variety which to my taste is much more beautiful than a complete mixture of whites and yellows. In the long borders under the terrace are more shrub roses, paeonies and cistus.

Before leaving the garden there are two other features which, for the energetic, are well worth a visit. To the north of the house is a magnificent stand of Douglas firs, some of the finest in the country and over 100 years old. When measured about ten years ago the tallest were 148 ft in height. A sign from the drive directs one to the willow garden around a pond to the north-east of the house. This is newly planted but since willows are very quick growing is already making a good spectacle. It is particularly interesting in early spring when the garden first opens and the catkins are golden and the foliage fresh and young but at any season it is worth a visit. It is surprising what a number of species there are and what

6 The trunks of *Myrtus luma* at Tresco Abbey, Isle of Scilly

7 A truss of *Rhododendron macabeanum* on the great tree at Trewithen, Grampound Road, Cornwall

variation they show.

By the drive there are groups of azaleas, unusually large oaks, *Q.robur* and *Q.petraea* and other good trees as well as masses of daffodils.

Everywhere visitors can tell what an active garden this is, always there are changes, always something new to see and learn. One visit is not nearly enough. We have indeed cause to be grateful to Sir John and Lady Amory for creating this masterpiece of a garden and to Lady Amory, Mr Hickson and the present staff for carrying it on in such good traditions and for the very high standard of its cultivation.

Marwood Hill

Dr J.A. Smart

4 miles N of Barnstaple, turn left signposted Marwood off B3230 Barnstaple–Ilfracombe. Entrance by nursery gate opposite Marwood Church. Open daily from 1 February–31 October in aid of National Gardens Scheme. House modern, not open. Choice nursery plants for sale with specialist collection of camellias. Young garden with lakes on steep sloping site begun in 1960 and made by present owner. Soil acid, rainfall heavy.

Marwood Hill is a garden of great interest containing a very varied collection of carefully selected and choice plants and has grown up well to give a feeling of maturity and form, although more planting is continually taking place. It also has two large glass houses filled with one of the finest collections of camellias in the country from which many prize-winning blooms are picked for the RHS camellia competition and show. Camellias from the collection are propagated and young plants are on sale at reasonable prices. So a visit even in February or early March is not too early to be rewarding. Here a number of the newer American hybrids of *Camellia reticulata* are being tested both in the greenhouses and outside.

From the greenhouses one can walk through into the main garden along a wide grass path beside a buttressed wall and look down towards the lakes. These were made by damming a small stream and filled in 1969. The whole looks very natural and the sides are well planted with moisture-loving plants. In early April the yellow *Caltha polypetala* was giving a great show. Everywhere on the slope are masses of daffodils making it a colourful garden at this season.

Some unusual tender plants have been placed under the wall on the south side, such as the mahogany-barked species of *Arctostaphylos* from the Pacific coast of North America, the very tender purple leaved *Dodonaea* and many others. The wall is 10 ft high and has been buttressed like the one at the Savill Gardens, providing extra protection and a grey upright conifer such as Juniperus 'Sky Rocket' has been very effectively placed against each buttress and a large collection of clematis has grown up, mostly to the top of the wall, especially the smaller flowered ones such as 'Etoile Violette', *C.texensis* 'Duchess of Albany' and the drooping bells of 'Gravetye Beauty'. The pink *Maurandia erubescens* was most effective as a climber and is rarely seen. So was a good *Mutisia oligodon*. Watsonias and other bulbs such as acidantheras nestled at the base and combined well with white Japanese anemones which were seeding into the wall. *Acacia pravissima* had made a good green mound in a sheltered corner and so has *Acacia verticillata*. Dr Smart has been most adventurous in his planting and it will be interesting to see what survives. This wall has become now one of the most interesting sections of the garden. Where the wall ends on the left is a rose garden with floribunda and hybrid tea roses to give mid-summer colour while on a small lawn beside the house is a 20 ft upright specimen of the fast-growing hybrid *Magnolia* x *loebneri* 'Merrill'. This was covered with creamy-white flowers early in April and seemed to me to be an unusually fine form. On the slope below the house beds have been planted with bulbs which appreciate summer warmth such as various watsonias from South Africa and the beautiful *Tulipa saxatilis* from Crete which surprisingly was flowering well. This is a lovely species with pale purplish-pink flowers and a deep yellow centre. On the house wall is a fine lobster claw plant *Clianthus puniceus* and Dr Smart told me that it flowered well. From here also one can look down over the garden and view the arrangement of the plants. A wide central grass path has a tall weeping silver pear in the centre at a cross junction and on each side of it are planted for contrast the red twigged maple *Acer* 'Senkaki'. This is a striking combination, especially good in winter when the maples give their best effect. There are large collections of magnolias, some of which have not yet reached their flowering stage but show promise of being magnificent in the future as one looks down on them. Embothriums flame like miniature fires in the early summer and rhododendrons have been chosen with discrimination. In early April there was a fine plant in flower of the Exbury-raised rhododendron 'Avalanche Alpine Glow' with large heads of scented pale pink flowers. Eucryphias are another feature of the garden and most of these have now reached flowering size and make a great feature in late July and August. At the west end of the lake a collection of willows has been planted and are mostly kept pollarded so as to produce plenty of young shoots. Particularly fine was a specimen of *Salix hastata* 'Wehrhahnii' by the water. This had abundant silvery grey round catkins on the stout young twigs. The planting round the lakes has rapidly become mature with pampas grass making great white plumes in late summer, striking focal plants when reflected in the water. The scarlet *Lobelia tupa* from Chile makes 5 ft spikes in great clumps while the bright blue *Salvia uliginosa* has grown 5 ft tall. Large groups of purple-leaved *Phormium tenax* and also the golden striped variety 'Veitchii' are often conspicuous plants around the water.

Another unusual feature was a thyme lawn between the two lakes, a mass of lilac-purple of varying shades as one looks down from above. In it dwarf bulbs have been planted, including dwarf narcissi collected by Dr Smart in Portugal.

On the far side of the lakes there is a collection of unusual ferns. The collection of hebes is also large with 'Amy', the very dark leaved variety standing out well. Towards the north of the house is a raised bed with dimorphothecas, gazanias, pink verbenas, *Fascicularia bicolor* and *Diplacus* (*Mimulus*) *glutinosus* in both dark red and apricot coloured forms and *Phlomis*. A collection of forms of variegated ivies is worth looking at by the garage.

If one follows the terrace walk along to the east end of the garden one comes to an old quarry. Recently this has been cleared of its coarse vegetation and rock-loving plants such as lewiseas placed in the crevices in the vertical positions in which they like to grow. The floor of the quarry has been covered with fine leaf mould and dog's tooth violets of various kinds planted in it. There is also an alpine scree with many plants collected in the wild. As these increase they should make a beautiful feature. On the banks at the further side of the lake a collection of unusual ferns and hostas is being made. New plantings are planned and will be made in 1977 of taxodiums and eucalyptus to round off the garden at the west end where more land has recently been taken in. Dr Smart is able to sit at the window of his drawing room and organise his garden as one might paint a picture. It is being most successful.

In general this is a garden of great variety with interest at all seasons although because of the exceptional collection of camellias many visitors will consider early spring the season. Dr Smart considers the peak season to be May with ceanothus, rhododendrons, magnolias, viburnums, cornus and other shrubs. Later there is a varied selection of clematis as well as plants such as *Mutisia oligodon, Dendromecon rigida, Callistemons* and *Cassia corymbosa*. It has been skilfully arranged and planted with many unusual plants. It is a connoisseur's garden. I know of few which have such large collections and which have been developed so quickly. Marwood Hill will surely reckon as one of the great gardens of the South-West.

Dr Smart writes in June, 1978, that he has recently turned over one of his camellia greenhouses to Australian plants which he collected on a recent visit and this promises to be a very interesting house.

Metcombe Brake

Mr and Mrs H.F. Weekes

At Higher Metcombe, $3\frac{1}{2}$ miles SW of Ottery St Mary, S of A30 by B3178 near Tipton St John. House not open. Woodland garden made by present owners during last forty years. Soil acid with much leaf-mould. Rainfall average for area.

Metcombe Brake is a medium-sized woodland garden with grassy glades stretching away from the house which has a fine *Camellia reticulata* 'Captain Rawes' on it while on the corner of the house is a good single form of the same camellia. It is a garden carpeted with daffodils, bluebells and heathers, delightful in spring. Two glades meet near the house and there is a large *Pieris floribunda* where they meet. The white tree heath *Erica arborea alpina* has grown very large and spreads freely but is very handsome in April. A pink cherry *Prunus sargentii* was also lovely then and gives good autumn colour. It is usually the first to colour. The beds are all curved at the edge giving an informal effect. Many rhododendrons have been grown from seedlings and from seed distributed by the Royal Horticultural Society. I noticed particularly a pink *R.orbiculare* with its bell-like flowers and rounded leaves, and also *R.oreotrephes* with its lilac flowers. Side paths deviate from the main glade and are worth following. A good group of a deep pink form of *R.albrechtii*, the azalea lay along one. In another direction was the pale yellow *R.lutescens* while *R.*'Loderi King George' had made a massive plant. *R.augustinii* was present in various shades as it comes from seedlings. An *Alnus incana*, the grey alder, was 30 ft. Heathers had spilled over onto the lawn and everywhere it was informal and charming.

Note: At time of second printing, June 1978, the garden was no longer open.

Powys, Sidmouth

Mrs Campbell-Watson

In Station Road, Sidmouth. Open for various charities, for date see local papers. A medium sized garden with some fine trees, made by a plant connoisseur. Soil acid and rainfall average.

Powys has six acres of delightful garden in the middle of Sidmouth and some rather unusual plants and some unusually fine trees. It is hoped that it may be preserved. On the lawn in front of the house is a fine cedar and an old sweet chestnut, also an old mulberry. In the grass daffodils have been planted in groups of a single variety. They always seem to me to look so much better in this way. The grass is kept mown in front of the house but otherwise in paths until after the daffodils have set their seed in June. Originally the garden was laurels and ivy, with the exception of the old trees. One enters by a large beech which now has primroses below. The natural grades well into the more formal part around the house, but nowhere is it very formal.

By the house a large mimosa *Acacia dealbata* flowers freely in very early spring. In a corner of the house is an unusual curly leaved laurel and underneath it *Stephanandra incisa* which bears panicles of greenish white flowers in June. In a warm border against a wall there was the finest *Corylopsis platypetala* that I have seen, not so vast as the great one at Trewithen, but covered with deep yellow flowers in hanging spikes. *Cassia corymbosa* shows how sheltered it is here and has grown well with orange flowers in summer. Watsonias from South Africa and the *Nerine bowdeni* flower well in autumn. *Clematis armandii* was covered with white flowers in April, beautifully trained against a wall. In a small greenhouse was the tender sweet-scented *Jasminum polyanthum*, one of the strongest scented of plants, also *Rhododendron cubittii*, one of the finest of the tender rhododendrons, and pelargonium 'Mabel Gray' one of the sweetest scented of the foliage ones. In a greenhouse which runs the length of the house were more, both the regal and the zonal pelargoniums in variety, the tender evergreen cultivars of *Rhododendron simsii*, beloved of florists. A cork oak *Quercus suber* was another unusual feature. Camellias and rhododendrons of many sorts were well represented and do well. The New Zealand *Sophora tetraptera* had made a small tree near the gate.

Rosemoor

*Col J.E. and The Lady Anne Palmer and Rosemoor
Garden Charitable Trust*

1 mile SE of Torrington on B3220 Torrington—Exeter. Garden sign-posted by bridge 1 mile from Torrington. Garden open daily dawn to dusk 1 April—31 October. Plants for sale. House not open. Teas available for groups by arrangement. Large garden of interesting trees and shrubs with primulas, alpines and other herbaceous plants started in 1959 by The Lady Anne Palmer. Heavy clay soil, acid. High rainfall, average 36—38 in. and humid atmosphere above River Torridge.

Rosemoor is an enthusiast's garden with a very large collection of carefully selected trees and shrubs and other choice plants integrated into an attractive setting sheltered from the north and east by a wooded hillside. Although comparatively recent it is already showing appreciable maturity and most of the plants have reached flowering size. It is well maintained and carefully planted. While probably its chief season is the spring, with rhododendrons and azaleas predominating, it is planned so as to give interest throughout the year, with some particularly good autumn colour.

One enters by the drive in front of the house. On the left in the bed in front of the house *Viburnum* 'Diane' is conspicuous in early April. This is regarded here and by many others as the finest of the hybrids of *V.carlesii* and shares its pink buds and scent. On the house and conservatory wall are a Banksian rose and *Ceanothus impressus* 'Puget Blue' which is covered with flower in late April and early May. It is one of the brightest blue of the early-flowering ceanothus.

In the lawn on the right is prunus 'Kursar' with deep pink flowers very early in the year. This was planted by that grand old veteran gardener Captain Collingwood Ingram who raised it. The garden owes much to his constant help and advice and to his generous gifts of plants.

Behind it is a long border with undulating edge running the length of the lawn. Here rhododendrons predominate but they have been generously interplanted with maples, magnolias, birches with ornamental coloured stems and cornuses. The magnolias include such early-flowering beauties as *M.campbellii*, its hybrid 'Charles Raffill' and *M.sprengeri diva*, all of which are about reaching flowering size. Opposite the house one should notice in late spring a good specimen of *Cornus capitata*, one of the most spectacular of the genus and also an unusual pink-flowering form of *Cornus kousa* raised by the late Norman Hadden at Porlock and possibly crossed with the Western American *Cornus nuttallii*. The shining creamy white trunk of *Betula ermanii* has been brought forward to the front of the border to break up the level of low planting there. Among the rhododendrons to be noted are good groups of the pink *R.spiciferum*, always sheared over after flowering, which keeps it compact, very deep purplish blue *R.russatum*, a lovely 'Crest', one of the finest yellows now available, a bank of *R.*'Calfort', raised by Collingwood Ingram from *R.calophytum* and *R.fortunei* with good foliage and large trusses of white flowers with a purple blotch. Another rarely seen but good hybrid is 'Thomasine' with bright pink flowers raised from *R.souliei* crossed with *R.thomsonii*. There are many others and they are well labelled. In groups towards the front primulas of many varieties and Ourisias, both white and red, have spread freely and made useful ground cover. It is unusual to see *O.coccinea* doing so well. In a bed on the lawn is a dwarf hybrid primula of the colour of a tomato with flowers almost of that colour. I have not seen it elsewhere and it was very effective and bright. At the end of the lawn is a large bed of brightly coloured deciduous azaleas, selected for their seedlings, with a background of *Eleagnus x ebbingei* which combines fast-growing with brightness from the silvery underneath of the leaves. At the back by the road are two tall trees of *Prunus yedoensis*, so beautiful in early April. In front of them is a bed with *Bergenias* for evergreen ground cover but also with pink or purple flowers in April and early May. Interspersed with it are irises for flower in late May and early June. Then one comes to a pond with mallard duck. On the bank are moisture-loving plants and near the drive is an unusually fine specimen of *Salix hastata* 'Wehrhahnii', covered with its round silvery catkins in early April. Beside it is *Eucalyptus viminalis*, the ribbon gum which sheds its bark in long ribbons. This is probably one of the tallest specimens in the county and although only planted nine years before was 35 ft in 1973.

As one proceeds down the drive there are some interesting

dwarf rhododendrons on the left such as *R.yakusimanum*, usually at its best in late May. Beyond is a small collection of white-stemmed birches bordering the drive while in the paddock on the left is a comparatively new planting of maples, sorbuses and other ornamental trees which will give great interest in the future. They are already beginning to show some of their features. There is also a fine old walnut while a background is given by conifers on the hillside.

Returning towards the house a hedge of *Eucalyptus gunnii* has been planted to disguise the hard tennis court and is kept topped at about 6 ft to increase the bushiness. This is both a decorative and effective arrangement. At the corners are some fine eucalyptus, *E.glaucescens* at one corner of the court and *E.perriniana* whose top is periodically cut off to encourage the rounded juvenile foliage. These were planted in 1964. Shrub roses are used plentifully in this area, lovely specimens of *R.alba* 'Celeste' grow well and are at their best in early July. This is surely one of the most beautiful combinations among roses between the pale blush pink flowers and the glaucous foliage. Both the red and the white forms of *Rosa paulii* have been pegged down on a bank to make good ground cover while with them are groups of the fine-foliaged *Viburnum davidii* and *V* 'Lanarth'. This part is well worth a visit in late June and early July. There is also a collection of *rugosa* roses. In May a fine *Embothrium*, the fire bush of Chile, is well placed against a green background of *Cupressocyparis leylandii*. Near here also is an unusual white *Rhododendron racemosum* at its best in late April.

Further up there is a small courtyard with a pillared building on the right reminiscent of the courts of Knossos in Crete and there are tubs and troughs with *Iris attica* and silvery *Euryops acraeus*. On the left is a combination very lovely in spring of the young foliage and red twigs of *Acer japonicum* 'Senkaki' and the pale plum-coloured leaves of *Paeonia mlokosewitschii* from the Caucasus and its delicate pale yellow globes of flower. On the right small peat walls and terraces are covered with choice dwarf rhododendrons of the *Saluenense* and *Lapponicum* series which have a long season of interest in April and May. Here can be seen a number of the most successful new dwarf yellow hybrids raised by Mr Peter Cox in Scotland such as 'Chikor' and 'Curlew' and at the top of the steps 'Chink' raised at the Savill Garden.

From the courtyard banks on each side of the path of large bushes of *Camellia japonica*, such as 'Mercury', and *C. x williamsii* very floriferous in April, lead up to the woodland garden and arboretum on the hillside. Much of this is comparatively young but growing fast. There are many good rhododendrons planted there. A large *Abies alba*, the silver fir, is a fine feature near the camellias. A grass bank above a small lane has been kept wild covered with primroses, wood anemones and violets and in late March and April is one of the loveliest sights in the garden.

One can then return to the house through the old kitchen garden under the wall. This has recently been redesigned and replanted with the help of Mr John Codrington, the garden architect. A large tulip tree has been underplanted with the pale blush primula 'Garryarde Guinevere' a distinctive plant with purplish foliage. Another great feature of this part is the beautifully polished mahogany trunk of a large tree of *Prunus serrula* well placed where the path forks. Here there are also large bushes of that excellent hybrid *Viburnum* x *burkwoodii*, 6 ft tall and covered with flower in April. There are useful dwarf willows, interesting through much of the year, both beside and in a large circular raised bed arranged by Mr Codrington to fit into the slope of the hill and surfaced with fine shingle. There are two smaller raised scree beds in front of the wall and in the bed under the wall are some unusual hebes (shrubby veronicas), olearias and cistuses. There is also a good prostrate rosemary with deep shrubby mauvy blue flowers while against the wall is the unusual and reputedly tender deep purple-leaved form of *Pittosporum tenuifolium* as well as the silver-leaved forms elsewhere. Nearer the house is a convenient herb garden arranged in little square beds with coloured paving between like a draught board. It is both decorative and a good practical arrangement since it keeps confined such persistent stragglers as the various mints and still allows enough for household uses.

As one moves out towards the greenhouse and sales area notice an unusual weeping conifer, a young tree of the rare *Fitzroya cupressoides* (*patagonica*) from South America, one of the pleasantest of the small drooping evergreens.

This is a garden full of surprises where one is likely to see the best both of the newer and the older shrubs, all beautifully maintained and labelled. It is a garden for all seasons and so well worth a visit at different times of the year. It is a garden where greater maturity will bring greater beauty from year to year, a garden still refreshingly full of new life and new plants.

Saltram

The National Trust

Near Plymouth, 3½ miles east of the centre of the city between A38 and
A379, 2 miles W of Plympton. Entrance signposted from roundabout
on A38 near Plympton. Gardens open daily November–March, from
1 April–31 October, 11 am–1 pm, 2–6 pm or sunset if earlier. House
also open. Restaurant. Given to the National Trust in 1957 by the
Treasury who had accepted it in lieu of death duties on estate of fourth
Earl of Morley. A large park with a garden of lawns, with some fine
trees and shrubs and paths through a woodland, largely planted by the
third Earl and Countess of Morley about a hundred years ago with
many subsequent additions. Soil acid. Rainfall average.

Saltram is a good example of a parkland surrounding a great house.
Originally the park was grazed with deer right up to the house in
the eighteenth century style but the National Trust in 1963
constructed a ha-ha to protect the lawns by the house and garden.

From the entrance one passes the south side of the house looking
across the lawn to magnificent views although the urban sprawl
and manufacturing area of Plymouth has much encroached on this.
The path leads round by the west side past four clipped upright
yews and on the left is an unusual clipped hedge of the evergreen
oak *Quercus ilex* about 30 ft in height. In July a *Rosa filipes*, one of
the most vigorous of climbing roses, grows up a tree close to the
hedge and cascades vast panicles of white flowers. A fine grey cedar
stands at the edge of the lawn and a path to the right leads down
between two herbaceous and shrubby borders to a decorative
white seat. Here are shrub roses at their best in June and July,
yuccas flowering in late summer with grey-leaved ballotas, silvery
blue leaved rue and white arums. On the left are some fine old
magnolias, *M.* x *soulangiana* 'Lennei' and *M.liliflora* 'Nigra'
flowering in late April and early May. They are backed by tall
Crinodendron hookeranum covered with the hanging red lanterns
against the dark evergreen foliage in late May and June. Here also
are bushes of the white *Staphylaea colchica* flowering earlier. The

path leads on past the gothicised chapel made from an old barn and then one reaches the magnificent orangery, one of the great features of the garden at Saltram. The Orangery, a large white building, is in classical style and was completed in 1775 and was made of wood. Unfortunately it was burnt in 1932 but restored by the National Trust in 1961 and now is one of the finest in the country. In front are two amusing lead sphinx. It is actually filled with large orange bushes in white Versailles-type tubs. They look very healthy and each summer they are taken out and stood in a circular enclosed area behind the chapel. This happens on oak-apple day, 29 May and then they are returned to shelter on the second Wednesday in October, the day of the Tavistock Goose Fair. With them are large tubs of agapanthus.

Their summer area has some notable plants around it, a very tall *Eucryphia cordifolia* with its white flowers in August, some old *Camellia japonica*, at their best in April but with a long spring season of flower, *Myrtus luma* (*apiculata*) shows its spectacular ochre bark and in April *Pieris japonica* will be covered with little white hanging bells like a lily of the valley. A background of fine beeches completes the picture. From here one can take a path through the woods to Fanny's Bower, a small Palladian temple with a grand view looking over the valley through the sloping woodland. This was the favourite seat of Fanny Burney, whose famous diary records a royal visit to Saltram in 1789. In early May the woodlands are carpeted with white garlic and bluebells.

Returning to the front of the Orangery one can keep on the path to the right passing a very fine Ilex evergreen oak and a large redwood (*Sequoia sempervirens*). A large *Halesia carolina* is particularly attractive in early May, dripping with white bells with an undercarpet of bluebells and behind a large whitebeam. Opposite are some large Japanese maples and some herbaceous and grey-leaved plants have been included for later summer effect. This is a rewarding path and passes some fine rhododendrons including R.'Loderi' and 'Lady Chamberlain', dripping with its pendulous orange bells in May. A large bush of the small-flowered white *Camellia cuspidata* is unusual and flowers early, while a large bush of *Eucryphia glutinosa* will be covered with white flowers in late July and August. In April the old bushes of *Camellia japonica* will show varying colours while later in the month and in early May a bank of the creamy *Cytisus* x *praecox* backed by a large ilex is a striking feature. Unusual also is a 25 ft specimen of the fine *Cornus capitata* from the Himalayas but it is growing now rather thin. By an enormous old bole of the sweet chestnut on the left of the path is *Rhododendron sinogrande* with its vast shiny leaves, sometimes 2 ft or more in length. Also notable here is a huge bush of *Parrotia persica* with its spreading horizontal branches, flaming bright orange-red in autumn, *Cercidiphyllum japonicum*, also superb in autumn, and the distinctive evergreen *Illicium anisatum* with its aromatic leaves and pale yellow flowers in spring. It comes from Japan and Formosa.

Then we come to the octagonal castellated summer house known as 'The Castle', from which a flag used to fly when the lord of Saltram was in residence. Near it are some very fine old trees, a vast spreading Lucombe oak, venerable old *Pinus radiata*, the Monterey pine, and, more unusual, a very tall stone pine *P.pinea*. Beds of shrubs to the left include some very fine blood red *Rhododendron arboreum*, 25 ft high and covered in early May with brilliant compact trusses of bright red flowers. There are also more large bushes of *R.'Loderi'*, one of the finest large-flowered hybrids covered with white or pale pink flowers in May, also many large maples.

From the focal point of the large Lucombe oak the lime avenue leads back to near the house. This is 260 yards long and is undoubtedly at all times of the year one of the particular glories of Saltram. In April the grass below is full of old white flowered narcissi and blue anemones while in the autumn there are masses of *Cyclamen neapolitanum* flowering abundantly from mid August; these have also naturalised themselves in other parts of the garden. Near the house end of the avenue on the left is a fine tree of *Acer griseum* with its peeling orange mahogany bark. Other successful combinations which I noticed in May included masses of the white daisy-like *Anthemis cupaniana* below the young yellow foliage of *Acer japonicum* 'Aureum', *Hydrangea quercifolia* with fine oak-like leaves with the wide-spreading *Aralia elata*.

Before one leaves it is worth looking at the bank of shrubs down the slope at the back of the house to see a large *Magnolia delavayi*, about 25 ft tall and 20 ft across, with its vast leathery leaves, and flowering usually from March–October. The flowers are large, creamy white but often partly hidden by the leaves and it is a plant usually grown for its foliage. Beside it is a silvery leaved *Eleagnus*.

Sharpitor (Overbeck's)

The National Trust

Near Salcombe, Devon, by A381 from Kingsbridge through Salcombe then 1½ miles SW of Salcombe near end of peninsular of Bolt Head, signposted from road by sea. Open: Garden daily throughout year; for details see 'National Trust Properties Open'. House Edwardian, Youth Hostel, not open to public, and museum of local interest open end March–end October. Garden of 6 acres made by the late Mr Otto Overbeck and bequeathed to National Trust in 1937. About 100 feet above sea level on shale, acid or nearly neutral soil. Almost free from frost, sheltered by surrounding trees and on sloping site protected from west winds, partly terraced. High rainfall, average 45 in. but also with good sunshine record.

Sharpitor is a unique garden with interest throughout the year and a number of old specimens of rare and tender trees. It is like a piece of Mediterranean coast with superb views down to the sea, through trees. One enters through a small avenue of palms (*Trachycarpus fortunei*) down a flight of steps, then turn right to terrace below the house, past a row of the evergreen Chilean lantern tree (*Crinodendron hookeranum*). The flowers are like little crimson Chinese lanterns and cover the bushes in late April and May.

The garden is on a steep wooded slope below the house with paths winding down and round, and a small terrace in front of the house extends along below the *Magnolia campbellii*. Another terrace facing south and south east with some more wide grass walks is above it and on a level with most of the branches.

Early March is not too early for a visit and then all eyes are drawn to the superb specimen of *Magnolia campbellii* on the middle terrace. It is a good deep pink form and, planted in 1901, is now about 40 ft tall and 45 ft across and bears its great chalices of flower by the thousand, a wonderful sight, especially if one is lucky enough to see it against a blue sky and with a blue sea below. It is certainly one of the finest specimens to be seen in any garden and very well placed. To the left of it is a large tree of the hybrid *Magnolia veitchii*, made from *M.campbellii* x *M.denudata*, and flowering several weeks later. Just beyond, also flowering in March, is an exciting combination of the yellow mimosa (*Acacia dealbata*) and the creamy white *Clematis armandii* covering the top of a high wall.

The terraces above the magnolia are well worth a visit and from here one gets a good view of it. In March there is a fine border of forms of the lenten hellebores (*H.orientalis*) along one side of this terrace. In the symmetrical beds of the terrace the large bushes of *Acacia verticillata* are notable. This is sometimes known as 'Prickly Moses' and flowers later than the ordinary mimosa. Against the wall are good plants of the red lobster claw *Clianthus puniceus* from New Zealand, a most spectacular plant when in flower in early summer. Close by is a good group of the red *Grevillea rosmarinifolia* flowering in March and April and looking like a rosemary although with bright crimson clusters of flower. It also comes from the Antipodes, from New South Wales. For early summer interest there are also here paeonies both herbaceous and the woody *P.delavayi* with its deep maroon flowers and in 1976 there was one of the tall echiums from Madeira in a very sheltered corner. This has blue spikes of flower up to 8 ft in a good specimen. In other years there may be more since they are usually treated as biennials and tend to spread from their own seedlings. Close by are various cistuses. In later summer there are masses of the deep pink *Amaryllis belladonna* 'Kewensis' and the distinct *Crinum bulbispermum* with pale blush pink flowers. This used to be known as *C.capense*.

On the terrace above this under the hillside is another of the great rarities of the garden the camphor tree, *Cinnamomum camphora*, a good 30 ft in height and nearly as much across. It is evergreen and the leaves when crushed smell strongly of camphor. The flowers in spring are small and greenish white. I know of no other specimen in English gardens nearly this size although Bean records that there used to be one at Penjerrick in Cornwall of 50 ft and one at Bicton in Devon of 35 ft, but both of these are now dead. Near it has been planted a young olive tree. Near it is also a large old tree of *Cornus capitata* and there are several others in the garden. This is the Himalayan species and very striking in June when the large sulphur yellow bracts subtend the inflorescence, four inches or so across. Later the fruits are crimson and strawberry-like.

As one returns towards the house one passes an enormous

Trochodendron aralioides, a tender evergreen with large leathery leaves not unlike those of a rhododendron and aromatic bark. The flowers are bright green in April and May. I have rarely seen so large a specimen and it has made a handsome tree. Even larger is a *Drimys winteri*, one of our finest foliage trees and flowering in early spring, and a very fine *Pittosporum eugenioides*, the tarata tree from New Zealand, also evergreen. The leaves are slightly waved at the edge and the flowers pale yellow in spring. Where the path branches is the Himalayan lilac, the unusual variegated form, *Syringa emodi* 'Variegata' whose leaves are bordered with yellow. It flowers in June. In a small bay on the terrace is an attractive and contrasting group of New Zealand flax, behind the tall *Phormium tenax* 'Veitchii' whose leaves are streaked with pale yellow and in front the purple-leaved *P. tenax* 'Purpureum' which does not usually grow so tall. This is a most useful combination. Opposite is an old bush of the *Fuchsia excorticata* with peeling bark and green and red flowers coming direct out of the branches. It comes from New Zealand. Nearer the house is a bay of *Yucca gloriosa* which has enormous spikes of white bells in late summer, while in the Conservatory before the house are several orange trees. Another feature of this area was a small border of *Anthemis cupaniana* which has bright silvery foliage and flowers almost throughout the season, beginning in March. The flowers are large white daisies about a foot high. There are sloping woodland paths slanting down the hill and here one passes more notable plants. Unusually large are two trees of the very prickly *Colletia cruciata* with its triangular spikes, grotesque plants, so well armed that one touches with caution. The flowers are greenish white in short clusters, petal-less, the effect being given from the sepal. They flower in late summer and early autumn. It is a native of Uruguay. Nearby there is a fine bush of the evergreen *Viburnum odoratissimum*, about 15 ft high and 20 ft across. It is one of the most handsome evergreens with large leathery leaves up to 8 in. long which often give good autumn colour. Its white flowers come in late summer followed by red fruits which later turn black. It is a native of China and India and is tender in most colder gardens. Near this is a fine young tree of *Acer distylum*, an unusual maple from Japan with leaves rather like those of a lime. As one goes down the hillside there are masses of hydrangeas for late summer and autumn colour and among them the rarer *H. quercifolia* with its decorative lobed oak-like foliage which give good autumn colour. Its flowers are white. Large areas are carpeted with the autumn-flowering *Cyclamen neapolitanum* with some of the largest leaves that I have seen anywhere. As one goes round the lower slopes towards the drive one passes some unusual shrubs, *Acacia melanoxylon*, 20 ft high, the blackwood from South Australia and Tasmania with pale yellow round heads in March. Close to the blackwood is another rarity *Rubia peregrina*.

In general this is a most interesting garden well worth a visit and it was good to see it tidy, well edged and cleaned up after a spell in which it became very overgrown. Also much new planting has been undertaken. It is a garden of great possibilities for the growing of tender plants and growth is rapid.

Slade

Mr and Mrs E.H. Hare

Near Cornwood, about 3 miles NW of Ivybridge. By A38 Exeter to Plymouth, leave mainroad at Ivybridge and proceed northwards at signs marked Cornwood. Garden open one Sunday in April and one in May, 2.30–6 pm in aid of selected charities. A medium-sized garden made largely by present owners and containing a good variety of choice plants. Soil neutral or slightly acid with some clay. Rainfall average for area.

Slade is in a fine position overlooking meadowland and river with distant views of Dartmoor and the house fits well into the landscape as if it had always been there. In fact the old barn is mentioned in Doomsday Book and the Barn Greeting Hall with Minstrel's Gallery dates back to the early thirteenth century. The garden contains a great variety of plants and is one for all seasons rather than a specialist's garden. All the plants would seem though to have been chosen and then placed with care. It is well sheltered from the east where lies Dartmoor and partly also from the north.

Near the entrance one notices a very good *Rhododendron thomsonii* with its dark red flowers in early spring. The garden is on sloping ground and has been divided into different compartments according to the land.

As one comes in one notices a lovely ceanothus 'Trewithen Blue' and many Japanese maples, which must be beautiful in the autumn. The polyanthus are the unusual Barnhaven strain bred so that there is no eye in the centre of the flower. The deep crimson forms look well in spring against the old stone walls. Magnolias have been planted freely and are now of flowering size. They include the pink form of *M.campbellii*, *M.sargentiana robusta* and *M. sprengeri diva* and a very good form of *M. x soulangiana* 'Lennei'. These are inter-mingled with azaleas and rhododendrons, flowering freely. A paddock with shrubs was planted 8 years ago, the top being planted for autumn colour effect. There are fine yew hedges, heavily cut back.

Cornus grows well here and I noticed a fine *Cornus florida* 'Rubra' followed in flower by a very big *Cornus capitata* whose sulphur yellow bracts surround the flowers in June and July when the roses are out. I also noticed a large *Gingko biloba* with beautiful foliage and for autumn colour both of fruit and foliage the thorn *Crataegus* x *lavallei* 'Carrieri'. In the walled garden was a very pale yellow *Iris innominata* hybrid obtained from Bressingham Gardens. A hedge of a good blue rosemary offset well the small-flowered but very sweet scented *Syringa microphylla* with its rosy-lilac flowers in June and sometimes as well intermittently throughout the summer.

An unusual feature is an old hornbeam hedge, perhaps 700 years old we were told and once known as a pleached alley. One side had been kept clipped, but the other had been allowed to grow. The branches are all twisted and gnarled and knobbly like a drawing by Arthur Rackham and most picturesque. A carpet of the beautiful pink *Erythronium revolutum* is below, nodding gently in the breeze. In the greenhouse is a China rose, possibly the originally intro-duced Old Blush China. There was also the loose growing but beautiful golden yellow rose 'Maréchal Niel', which was raised in France in 1864. The buds are long and pointed and the scent good, but it is rarely seen now.

The Gardens of Cornwall

Antony House

The National Trust and Sir John Carew Pole, Bt

5 miles W of Plymouth via Torpoint Car Ferry, off A374 2 miles NW of Torpoint. National Trust; open April to September inclusive Tuesday, Wednesday, Thursday and Bank Holiday Mondays 2–6 pm. House also open. A garden round a historic house looking down to the Lynher River, an estuary of the River Tamar. Also a Woodland Garden owned by the Antony Charitable Garden Trust – open from the middle of March until the end of May. Plant Centre – plants for sale. Open daily except Saturdays. Soil acid in Woodland Garden, clay with shillet and leaf mould. Rainfall average for area. There are two car parks – one for the National Trust visitors to the House and Garden, the other in close proximity to the Wild Woodland Garden and Plant Centre. Both are indicated by signs.

The gardens at Antony House can well be divided into two. The Wild Woodland Garden was started in a dense wood in 1938, left unattended during six years of war and restarted in 1947. Only about half a dozen plants survived the war years. This garden is now open on behalf of the Antony Garden Charitable Trust. The garden around the House and stretching down to the lawn to the north is open with the House by the National Trust.

To enter the Woodland Garden you proceed towards the Plant Centre as indicated by direction signs and here there is a car park. At the entrance of the Woodland Garden you walk along a cut grass path through the small plantation of Norway spruce, following direction signs you bear left above the valley with camellias and rhododendrons on each side of the path. Near the top before reaching the gate there are great blocks of *R.griffithianum* hybrids raised by Sir John, among them some specially good ones both white and pink. Here you find a path leading down to the valley. A small stream flows down through the valley and the trees have been thinned to provide space for the plantings which in their turn have become tree like. A background of older trees has, however, been left on both sides.

Camellia sasanqua in great variety begin to flower in early November and continue throughout the winter to be followed by *Camellia* x *williamsii* and *C.saluenensis* and *C.japonica* in spring, many of which are available from the Plant Centre. Everywhere there are masses of bluebells, pink campions and cow parsley. Magnolias abound. A young plant of *Magnolia campbellii alba* has been planted at the top with an old wall as background and of flowering size are *M.campbellii*, the deep pink form and behind it is a large *Davidia involucrata*. As one goes further down there are *Magnolia* 'Charles Raffill' and *M.sprengeri diva*, *M.dawsoniana* and several plants of *M.mollicomata* including the dark purple 'Lanarth' and *M.sargentiana* var. *robusta*. A vast plant, perhaps 60 ft tall of *M.* x *veitchii*, the white 'Isca' form, was planted in 1948 and flowers freely. *Michelia doltsopa* has made another large plant and flowers well each year, the rusty fur-covered buds opening into great creamy blooms.

Rhododendrons have flourished. The scent of the great white trumpets of *R.lindleyi* is wafted towards one, planted in large groups, mostly the hardier form, collected by Ludlow and Sheriff and grown in Mr Gibson's garden at Rhu, Dunbartonshire. *R.yunnanense* billows out in masses of flower in May while *R.macabeanum*, a group grown from seed of the great tree at Trewithen, is at its best in March and early April. *R.sinogrande* was one of the first rhododendrons to be planted here and is a fine white-flowered form as indeed are many of the Cornish ones as opposed to the Scottish ones which have more cream in their flowers. The young leaves are very fine; silvery below and powdered green above and vast in size.

The path leads down to the water where there are some very large *Pinus radiata* and new plantings are being made consisting of rhododendrons and a considerable variety of shrubs, some of which should in addition provide good autumn colouring. A group of the tender large-leaved *R.giganteum* has been made. Here its pinkish-purple flowers come in March. A glade of *R.luteum* with white garlic below is beautiful both in May and October.

There is also a third woodland garden at Antony House. It is called the Wilderness and is of considerable acreage but is not open to the public except on special occasions, chiefly for the benefit of charities. This is situated below the National Trust lawns to the north west of the House in the woods leading down to the river. This garden consists of a large variety of long established species and hybrid rhododendrons many of which were raised at Exbury.

Camellias also abound including a considerable number of up to date American plants – *williamsii*, *reticulata*, *japonica*, *saluenensis* and many others. There is also a wide choice of interesting shrubs, trees and magnolias. *Olearia cunninghamii* and *Drimys winteri* var. *latifolia* have both made fine specimens. The evergreen azalea 'Apple Blossom' contrasts well with pale blue *Rhododendron augustinii* and yellow *R.triflorum* while earlier there is *R.lutescens* and masses of **Myrtus lechlerana. Walks are kept cut through the long grass.** *Cornus florida rubra* flowers well and so does *Magnolia x veitchii*. A tree of the white-stemmed *Pinus bungeana* is unusual.

Returning to the National Trust lawns in front of the house there are some old ilex probably planted about 1750 soon after the house was built. A plant of *Ulmus viminalis* with feathery green foliage is near the path, a species rarely seen. Higher up are two fine tulip trees, which flower freely. But most unusual on the lawn is the specimen of the Shagbark hickory *Carya ovata*. This is reputed to be the largest in the country and is 55 ft tall and 81 ft in diameter and was planted about 150 years ago. It is mentioned in Alan Mitchell's *Field Guide to Trees of Great Britain and Northern Europe*. It comes into leaf late but colours well in the autumn. A big cedar is to the left, probably about as old as the house. Rose 'Iceberg' has been planted in a long bed in front of the house. To the left of the house are two long terraces backed by clipped yews of great age. Along one *Magnolia denudata* has been planted and on the other *M.grandiflora*, the evergreen species. Unfortunately most unusual late frosts browned the former in 1975 and 1976. Against the end of these terraces are two little Japanese granite lanterns brought from Japan at the beginning of this century and a very large bell brought from Burma in the late nineteenth century. On the upper terrace is a wonderful specimen of the cork oak *Quercus suber*, the largest that I have ever seen. It was also measured for Alan Mitchell's book at 62 ft tall with a girth of 15 ft and I paced it at 27 yd across.

Finally we must mention the hemerocallis, the day lilies, which were Lady Carew Pole's speciality. A collection of the finest is planted **round the courtyard as one enters the house and other cultivars have been planted in suitable places in the garden. They are at their best in July and August, when the rhododendrons are over.**

Caerhays Castle

F. Julian Williams Esq

About 8 miles SW of St Austell, by B3273 to Mevagissy and along coast or from Truro by A390 and A3038 branching off at Tregony for three miles through lanes, signposted. Garden open on Easter Sunday and on one Sunday earlier in May in aid of local charities. Large woodland garden of camellias, magnolias and rhododendrons made by the late J.C. Williams from 1897. Soil acid. Rainfall high.

Caerhays has a large collection of rare and in some cases unique trees and shrubs built up largely by seedlings from the great collections in Western China and by hybrids raised by Mr J.C. Williams and his successors. He was the chief sponsor of the Forrest expeditions and also subscribed to Wilson, Farrer and Kingdon-Ward expeditions. The garden is about 100 acres in extent and is planted in an open woodland on the side of a hill and stretching down nearly to the sea on one side. It is protected from the north and east by hills behind and is very mild. The plants were placed in the areas where it was thought that they would do best; as they grew and the woodland was thinned to make space they tended to make their own microclimate around them. It has specialised in three genera, *Magnolia, Rhododendron* and *Camellia* but collections of other trees such as oaks are grown. As one ascends the hillside past the castle it is better to follow the arrows put out for the occasion along the paths cut through the long grass, pausing as one goes along. No map can readily be drawn. For instance the *Magnolia* x *veitchii*, has grown to about 85 ft and dominates the lower part of the garden and is a fine sight when in flower. It was planted in 1921. The other magnolias of this section grown include both the pink and the white forms of *M.campbellii, M.campbellii mollicomata* in various forms. *M.sprengeri diva, M.sargentiana robusta* and *M.dawsoniana*. When seen in flower between late February and April they are truly magnificent and probably no plants in the garden can equal them when covered with flowers. Some have grown to 40 or 50 ft in height and bear thousands of flowers. Most have been allowed to grow naturally, branching from the base. My favourites among them are probably the white *campbellii*, the flowers of which may reach 8 in. or more across and the glorious pink *M.sprengeri diva*, when seen against a blue sky. Many seedlings have been raised and distributed and also many intentional hybrids have been raised, *M.sargentiana robusta* x *mollicomata*, *M.sprengeri diva* x *M.sargentiana robusta*, *M.campbellii* x *M.mollicomata* and these are now beginning to flower well and awards have been won by several. 'Caerhays Surprise' was raised here but 'Kew's Surprise' was raised by C.P. Raffill of Kew but grown at Caerhays. Both of these plants have won the Cory cup in recent years. 'Caerhays Surprise' is *M.mollicomata* x *M.* x *soulangiana* 'Nigra', a good April flowering dark magnolia with the influence of both plants clearly discernable in the flowers and the growing habits of both its parents. 'Kew's Surprise', a cross between *M.campbellii* x *mollicomata*, has dark red flowers — but not in the same class as 'Lanarth'. These plants it is hoped will be a valued addition to many gardens. The later flowering ones are also grown well. Along the sea wall the large-leaved *M.delavayi* has recently had to be trimmed since it was getting too high, but is still a fine sight. In the wood it is even larger. *M.rostrata* grows well to 35 ft and the flowers appear among the vast leaves in June. *M.sinensis* and *M.wilsonii* hang their white flowers. The Michelias have grown equally well, although are more tender. *M.doltsopa* is probably the finest with its furry covered ends and creamy sweet scented flowers. As one wanders up the hill along the grass paths it is like a voyage of exploration and one can imagine oneself in the Himalayas or the Chinese Alps, only one sees the plants of many hundreds of miles gathered together into one or two.

Rhododendrons include many hybrids raised from *R.arboreum* such as 'Red Admiral' (*arboreum* x *thomsonii*) and many hybrids from the Maddenii Series such as the lemon coloured 'Michael's Pride' named after the late head gardener Charles Michael, 'Caerhays John', a lovely deep yellow, and 'Caerhays Philip', deep buff orange at base and paler towards its tip. The large-leaved rhododendrons are particularly fine. A form of *R.sinogrande* with very yellow bells is outstanding and so is *R.falconeri* x *R.macabeanum* but *R.falconeri* x *R.lacteum* has not yet flowered but promises to be a good plant. One of the most successful seedlings raised here is 'Yellow Hammer', (*flavidum* x *sulfureum*) and it hardly ever seems to out of flower, a thicket 14 yd long × 10 ft tall. A group of *R.*

williamsianum x *R.callimorphum* was raised at Caerhays, a deep pink bell and seems particularly nice. Another very fine *williamsianum* hybrid was a cross with *martinianum*. 'Lady Alice Fitzwilliam' has made a bank 15 ft high and scented the air around. *R.zeylanicum* x *griffithianum* had a wonderful red glow as one looked up at the flowers. *R.orbiculare* x *R.decorum* was a good pink. Earlier flowering hybrids include 'Golden Oriole Talavera' probably the best yellow yet derived from *R.moupinense* and quite hardy at Caerhays. Another large-leaved one is 'Assaye' (*calophytum* x *sutchuenense*) with blush pink flowers very early in the year. *R.williamsianum* arrived from the Arnold Arboretum about 1913 and is now 36 ft across and 8 ft tall, quite large for a plant often described as a dwarf. *R.crassum* has made a bank 20 ft long. A white *R.stamineum* is a plant not often seen.

Camellias are equally good. The original bank of the *williamsii* hybrids such as 'J.C. Williams', 'Mary Christian' and 'St Ewe' still survive and are still unsurpassed, but others have been raised more recently and include some double ones such as 'George Blandford' and 'Caerhays' and that floriferous deep pink single 'Rosemary Williams'. The paler pinks include 'Beatrice Michael' and 'Charles Michael'. 'Cornish Snow', raised from *C.saluenense* x *C.cuspidata* makes up by its abundance of flower for the size of them and can be regarded as one of the best Caerhays hybrids. Finally *C.reticulata* 'Captain Rawes' has made several vast plants throughout the garden.

But in addition to these three genera there are many other plants of interest. There is a large collection of oaks and *Lithocarpus*. I particularly noted *Lithocarpus pachyphylla*, *Quercus velutina* and *Q.lamellosus* 35 ft high. *Emmenopterys henryi* is now about 50 ft tall, but still has not flowered. Wilson described it as likely to be China's best gift to English gardens. The young foliage, however, is decorative. *Hartia sinensis* and *Tetracentron sinense* at 30 ft are unusual. *Aesculus wilsoni* flowers in June and is enormous, a tree not often seen. *Lindera megaphylla* is an unusual plant with long narrow leaves. The nothofagus are good. *N.procera* has reached about 100 ft and there are also *N.obliqua* and *N.menziesii*. But one could go on for ever in detailing plants from this vast treasure chest, presided over so ably by Mr Julian Williams and his head gardener Mr Philip Tregunna.

Carclew

Judge and Mrs Chope

Off A39 Falmouth–Truro, about 4 miles south of Truro turn left, then signposted. Garden open in aid of local charities several Saturdays in April and May, 2–6 pm and by special arrangement on request. House not open. Garden made on site of old Carclew mansion garden. Soil an acid loam. Rainfall about 50 in. Climate very mild owing to tidal water of River Fal. In top garden by house limy owing to old kitchen garden.

One enters the garden under an old beech tree at the base of the garden. It was originally made by Sir Charles Lemon who was a friend of Joseph Hooker and an original seedling of *Rhododendron falconeri* grown from his seed stands in the garden. It is now vast but still in good health. Here also was grown that fine form of *R.arboreum*, known as 'Sir Charles Lemon' with the rusty underside to the leaf. Sir Charles Lemon's mansion house, then described as the finest Palladium mansion in Cornwall, was burnt down in 1934 and later a new house was built by Mr Jack Silley on a new site at the top of the present garden, from which the old rhododendrons are a staggering sight. He largely developed the present garden with its series of terraces but it has been ably carried on by Judge and Mrs Chope. The site of the old house now lies outside the garden. There is also a Lucombe oak, a good tree with a straight stem which could date from Sir Charles Lemon's day. It is at least 100 ft high and there is a story that one of the two forms arose at Carclew in 1765, the other at Lucombe. The one at Cardew had pale grey fissured bark and long leaves. There is also an old *R. griffithianum* and a vast bank of that variable hybrid 'Cornish Red' which dominates the garden.

One of the features of the garden is the great lily pond with swans which eagerly scurry over its surface and fountains which still play. It was a great day when the swans arrived by rail in a box. There is a little temple beside the pond. Around it are banks of rhododendrons, notable among which is the rare *R.araiophyllum* of the Irroratum Series, an almost flat white flower with darker blotch. There are also 'Gill's Goliath', big loderis, *R.eximium* with its rusty leaves below and many others. As one goes up the hill one passes a large bank of *R.*'Fragrantissimum' smelling so sweet that the Judge said that it was almost a pleasure to mow the lawn above it. A little viewpoint, approached beside a large mahonia, is a good point to rest a minute. A big *Ginkgo biloba* stands out by the pond.

As one ascends the terraces there are two big *Camellia reticulata* 'Captain Rawes' on the wall and on the terrace of the middle lawn a fine tall urn and a wisteria along the wall. Contrasting with golden yew are purple-leaved berberis and maples and very fine *Viburnum davidii* with decorative foliage. A very pretty round lily pond occupies one terrace and another has rose beds and fine stone balustrading. There is a large *Phlomis fruticosa*, a big *Magnolia* x *soulangiana* and a handsome *Pieris formosa* by a *Hydrangea petiolaris*, while up one side of the terraces are tall *Prunus* 'Amanogawa'. Beside the top lawn *Paulownia tomentosa* flowers in late May and there is also the double white gean.

On the house *Rosa* x *anemonoides* 'Ramona' flowers early above an *Azara*, there is also *Abutilon megapotamicum* while by the front door is a good *Pieris forrestii*. On the wall by the entrance are romneyas and honeysuckles and by a decorative marble frieze of bambinos is *Sollya drummondii* with its little blue bells.

Further details on the history of Carclew can be found in the issue of Country Life for 14 April, 1934, just before the fire, when the house belonged to Captain Charles H. Tremayne, a descendant of Sir Charles Lemon.

I found this one of the most pleasing gardens in Cornwall with its successful combination of the formal and informal, as well as the fine plants.

Chyverton

Mr and Mrs Nigel Holman

N of A30, 1 mile SW of Zelah. Turn off A30 at signpost Zelah. About
6 miles N of Truro. Garden open in aid of Charity 2–5.30 pm on at
least one Sunday in May and on other occasions by special arrangement.
House not open. Large garden of rhododendrons, camellias and magnolias in which Mr Holman specialises. Soil very acid, loam and shale.
Rainfall average 40 in.

The garden at Chyverton was laid out originally by John Thomas at
the end of the eighteenth century and then carried on by Mr
Holman's father in 1930 and later by himself and his wife. There
is a magnificent view from the house over the valley to where a
small stream was dammed in 1830 to make a broad expanse of
water bordered by gunneras and lysichitums, and on the far side
Rhododendron 'Cornish Red', planted about 1870. Opposite the
front door there is a wonderful dark mauve form of *Rhododendron
augustinii* and in front of it the yellow *R.*'Marcia' and *R.cinnabarinum
roylei*. Then came a tall *Eucalyptus nicholsii* raised in 1966 from
Australian seed by Mrs Holman's father Mr E.F. Lole, a delicate
and graceful species. On the wall facing north is one of the great
rarities of the garden, *Magnolia nitida*, a tender species, 14 ft in
height and bearing a few of its creamy pale yellow flowers. The
young leaves are a shining purple-brown, hence its name *nitida*,
shining. There is also a large *Berberidopsis corallina*, the coral plant
of Chile with its deep crimson flowers. On the side of the drive is
Rhododendron quinquefolium with its hanging white flowers and an
old copper beech planted in 1730 when the house was built, behind
it is a fine cedar of Labanon. An unusually fine form of *Rhododendron
schlippenbachii*, in a large planting of this beautiful deciduous species
with flowers floating on the bare branches like large butterflies,
was much praised by the late Rosa Harrison, a noted authority on
the species of rhododendron, and is worth looking out for. Above
the group is a tree of *Styrax obassia* with large white bells hanging
in June, one of the finest species of this genus.

Below the house is a 12 ft hedge of *Myrtus luma* (*M.apiculata*), its cinnamon peeling bark shining in the sunlight and a hedge of *Leptospermum flavescens* about the same height. Below is a group of *Viburnum plicatum* 'Mariesii' and the snowball tree *V.plicatum tomentosum*. A seedling of *Magnolia sprengeri diva* competed with a large *Halesia carolina* with its snowdrop bells and a group of forms of *Camellia* x *williamsii* for interest. A young *Magnolia cylindrica* flowers well near here and may well turn out to be even a better plant than *M.denudata*. *Rhododendron* 'Charles Michael' (*burmanicum* x *dalhousiae*) was beautiful with its large greenish yellow trumpets but alas it is too tender for most gardens. Beside it *Edgeworthia papyrifera* could be tied into knots, so flexible are its branches. It is a close relation of the daphnes. Then we come to a large plant of *Schima khasiana* a relation of the camellias from the Himalayas with white flowers in autumn and *Michelia doltsopa*, also tender but here producing its white flowers. Below it as one proceeded downhill was a very large *Pieris forrestii* 25 ft tall and a *Rhododendron edgeworthii*, a very fine pink-flowered form.

Then we come to some fine magnolias, *M.hypoleuca*, spreading scent strongly from large white flowers, *M.* x *soulangiana*, *M. campbellii*, *M.globosa*, the Chinese form, and lower down the slope the Indian form which flowers later than the Chinese form which used to be called *M.tsarongensis*. *Rhododendron burmanicum* 'Lanarth', pale yellow is a good clone of this species, over it spreads *Prunus* 'Shirofugen'. *R.anwheiense*, a rare species from West China, looked not unlike *R.yakusimanum* but as it develops will grow taller and less compact. Two trees of *Magnolia sargentiana robusta* complete a lovely picture in early spring. The large leaves of *R.macabeanum* x *magnificum* as yet unflowered promise a most interesting plant and so does *R.arizelum*, a tree of George Forrest's collecting, very rusty on the underside of the leaf.

A small path to the left passes a very large *Cupressus macrocarpa* which has been opened up to allow space for eucalyptus, *E.regnans*, *E.delegatensis* and several others. *Pinus patula* from Mexico with long drooping bright green needles has made several trunks and is now 30 ft tall. An enormous Norway maple is beyond it. *Magnolia campbellii alba* was planted in 1953 and is well placed against a dark background. It has flowers 17 in. across when fully open and flowered in 13 years from seed. Other good magnolias are *dawsoniana*, 45 ft tall, and good all round, 'Chyverton' raised here and now established as a form of *M.dawsoniana* and about 50 ft tall, an Award of Merit plant, and a large group of *M.stellata* with *Rhododendron* 'Cornish Red' behind. There is a big spreading *Davidia involucrata* and a nice specimen of *Styrax japonica*. *Malus* is also well represented with *M.hupehensis* (*M.theifera*) very pretty against the blue sky, a large tree good both in flower and fruit, and *M.baccata* the Siberian crab, collected in Manchuria by Collingwood Ingram. *Betula ermanii* has fine white bark, a species which should be planted more often. Large-leaved rhododendrons are well represented, *R.sinogrande*, the form with whitish rather than yellowish flowers has grown into large bushes, *R.giganteum* x *R.magnificum* from seed from Brodick Castle in Scotland. *R.macabeanum*, a good form with large yellow bells, and *R.macabeanum* x *R.sinogrande*, with a large yellow truss are all represented. I also noted an interesting seedling of *Magnolia sargentiana* x *mollicomata*. *Drimys winteri* with waxy-white flowers in summer is unusually large, and striking in its young copper-tinted growth is *D.lanceolata* (formerly known as *D.andina*). The striking trunks of *Betula albosinensis* have a white bloom with a terracotta tinge hard to describe while *B.jacquemontii* stands out for its dazzling whiteness. A large area of *Rhododendron griersonianum* is staggering in its brilliance of geranium-red flowers in June while other plants worth looking at include the weeping form of *Podocarpus salignus* from Chile with its elegant foliage and sorbus 'Mitchellii' one of the most handsome of the whitebeams with very large leaves. Coming back to the house was a *Quercus pubescens*, also enormous, a tree close to the Durmast oak but with greyer and more downy leaves. Altogether this is a very interesting and rich collection and well worth a visit at more than one season.

Chyverton is particularly notable for its magnolias which Mr Holman's father planted with gay abandon in the late 1940's and early 1950's to use the present owner's words. He reckoned that they had over 100,000 blooms of the Yulan Magnolias.

Cotehele

The National Trust

On west bank of River Tamar, 6 miles west of Calstock, SW of Tavistock by A390 and then signposted. Garden open daily, November–
March during daylight, end of March–end October 11 am–1 pm and
2–6 pm. House also open. Restaurant. A garden made round the old
mediaeval house and an informal woodland garden stretching down
to the River Tamar, mostly facing north. Soil mostly acid. Rainfall heavy.

The grey granite walls of Cotehele make a fitting background for
many good plants. *Schizandra rubrifolia*, *Viburnum rhytidophyllum*
and the yellow *Jasminum mesnyi* (better known as *J.primulinum*) all
revel against them. The large decorative leaves of the viburnum,
puckered on top, one seldom sees in so good a setting. Cotehele
has a clever combination of rather formal courtyards with
pomegranates and myrtles and informal plantings as one goes
down the valley. If one turns right to the east front of the house one
comes to a fine terrace dominated by two fine magnolias, *M.
soulangiana*, one is the pink 'Rustica Rubra', the other 'Alba
Superba'. The terrace beds are full of roses, the upper one under-
planted with silver leaved lamb's tongue (*Stachys lanata*), the lower
with aubrieta. It makes a fine sight in May. The borders under the
walls have yellow *Phlomis fruticosa*, the green *Euphorbia characias*
which combines so well with stone, yuccas and rues contrasting
with dark purple-red leaved *Cotinus coggygria*, *Magnolia grandiflora*
with its handsome evergreen foliage contrasted with the silver of
Cytisus battandieri. This comes from Morocco and its flowers in June
smell strongly of pineapple. A white wisteria covers another wall.

Down the valley we come to a most decorative dovecote with a
pond in front and white arums at the edge. The dovecote is one of
the largest I have seen. Clever use has been made of the St John's
Wort *Hypericum calycinum* to cover the steep banks. A nice plant of
Magnolia sinensis for late May-flowering decorates the side on the
left. The heather 'W.T. Rackcliff' has grown to 3 ft round the pond

1. Bicton, near Budleigh Salterton: part of the formal Italianate garden.

2. Bicton: part of the pinetum.

3. Cotehele: the old dovecote with ornamental pond beside.

4. Castle Hill, near Barnstaple: part of the view from the front of the house showing one of the stone lions and also a very good urn.

5. Endsleigh arboretum, near Tavistock: the terrace designed by Humphrey Repton.

6. Endsleigh: A tall weeping beech in the arboretum.

7. Endsleigh: *Pinus montezumae.*

8. The Garden House, Buckland Monachorum: *Clematis indivisa* from New Zealand, a rare clematis to see outside even in a sheltered corner.

9. Buckland: part of the old tower and the lowest herbaceous and shrub border.

10. Killerton: trunks of
the surviving cork oak,
Quercus suber.

11. Killerton: *Magnolia
kobus* hybrid near the
entrance.

12. Knightshayes Court, near Tiverton: the long walk with raised beds for choice alpines.

13. Knightshayes: the pool garden.

14. Marwood Hill, near Barnstaple: part of one of the pools with the bank leading up to the wall behind. Pampas grass makes a fine focal point reflected in the water.

15. Saltram: part of the avenue. It is underplanted with old daffodils for flower in spring and cyclamen in autumn. At the end is a Turkey oak.

16. Sharpitor: part of the *Magnolia campbellii* in flower in March.

17. Antony House: looking towards the house from the end of the lawn.

18. Antony House: *Carya ovata*, the Shagbark hickory, an old and rarely seen tree.

19. Carclew Garden, between Truro and Falmouth: old rhododendrons. In the foreground is *Rhododendron falconeri*, a large-leaved species probably grown from Sir Joseph Hooker's original seed.

20. Carclew Garden: old 'Cornish Red' rhododendrons around ornamental pond and the fountain.

21. Carclew: looking down on old rhododendrons.

22. Glendurgan: *Agave americana* with flower spike on lawn. Mrs Helen Fox, the former owner of the garden, stands beside it.

23. Glendurgan: a very old tulip tree in spring, with rhododendrons behind and bluebells below.

24. Lamellen, near Wadebridge, a garden where many good rhododendrons were raised. The light one is called 'Lamellen' after the garden.

25. Tremeer, St Tudy, a garden where General Harrison has specialised in raising bright violet-blue rhododendrons. He also grows camellias in large quantities: 'Donation' is shown on the right.

26. Lanhydrock House: tree magnolias in flower on the hillside.

27. Penjerrick House, where many famous rhododendrons were raised including 'Penjerrick' and 'Cornish Cross'. A fine weeping beech is in the background.

28. Trengwainton House: a veteran tree of *Rhododendron falconeri*.

29. Tresco Abbey, Isles of Scilly: part of the palm walk, leading up to the Neptune Steps. A fine *Furcrea bedinghausii* is in flower on left; in centre, two royal palms: on right the mass of *Metrosideros tomentosa*, the rata of New Zealand.

30. Trewithen: top of the great lawn looking away from the house.

31. Trewithen: *Rhododendron macabeanum*, by many considered the finest specimen in the country. The flower is a deep yellow.

and is interspersed with *Potentilla fruticosa* both yellow and the creamy 'Primrose Beauty'. Unfortunately the valley is rather a frost pocket, facing north-east. Cotehele in this respect is a surprisingly cold garden. A very large *Davidia involucrata* had been completely frosted in the spring of 1976. With it were tall yellow *Rhododendron campylocarpum* and some old Cornish hybrid rhododendrons. It is a pleasant walk down the valley through the woods to a little chapel and the old quay. On the way back notice a tall *Embothrium*, the Chilean flame tree behind a large *Cornus capitata*, perhaps the finest of the dogwoods and also fine old purple-leaved Japanese maples underneath.

On the upper terrace *Hydrangea villosa* occupies a bay in the wall and flowers in late summer. *Camellia sasanqua* for autumn flowering is also on the house and a yellow Banksian rose towers over it. By the front door there are ceanothus which are covered with flower in May. The top courtyard has *Abelia floribunda* with its tubular magenta-red flowers in June, a most effective shrub. *Myrtus communis* gives a touch of the Mediterranean while *Hydrangea petiolaris* clings to the walls. More camellias are lovely there in early spring, the hybrid 'J.C. Williams', one of the most beautiful ever raised with its single pale pink flowers and 'Cornish Snow', with masses of little white flowers. Then we come out to a meadow with daffodils growing in the long grass, lovely in the spring, and Judas trees, *Cercis siliquastrum*, flowering well.

There is a paddock with a vast tulip tree effective against the background of the house. A lily pond and a herbaceous border with large acanthus makes a good summer picture. A gold ash *Fraxinus excelsior* 'Aurea' (or 'Jaspidae') is in the upper garden by a small pond. On the way out there are some good trees in the avenue, mostly sycamores. A fine *Podocarpus salignus* stands above the bowling green.

County Demonstration Garden and Arboretum

Near Probus on A390, 8 miles E from Truro. Formerly part of the Trewithen estate. Garden open: October–April, Thursdays 2–5 pm; May–
September, daily 2–5 pm, but Thursdays 2–8 pm and Sundays 2–6 pm.
Advisor on duty in demonstration garden on Thursdays. Soil largely
made up to suit requirements. Average rainfall.

This consists of 41 different small plots and gardens set up by the
County Horticultural Adviser to demonstrate what can be done in a
small garden in Cornwall. The site is open and exposed to wind, but
so are the majority of small gardens in Cornwall. It is designed to
demonstrate what can be grown on various sites and soils and in
this way should be a great help to gardeners in the county. There
are gardens for acid and limey soils, labour saving gardens, patio
gardens, shrubs for walls, demonstration plots for fruit and vege-
tables, based on the RHS Vegetable Garden Displayed and the
Fruit Garden Displayed. There is an interesting section devoted to
plants which have originated in Cornish gardens such as Camellia
'J.C. Williams' and *Ceanothus* 'Trewithen Blue' and plants arranged
in chronological order by date of introduction from Roman times.
There are plots of roses arranged to show results of different methods
of pruning and feeding and also a historical collection of roses
showing the more important groups such as moss, china, musk,
cabbage roses, etc. Emphasis is laid on plants which do particularly
well in Cornwall such as hydrangeas, heathers, hardy fuchsias,
carnations and pinks, bamboos, eucalyptus, and there are various
garden layouts for labour-saving gardens, plantsman-gardens and
gardens to achieve 'tropical' effect making use of cordylines, New
Zealand flax and similar plants. There are suitable plants for
hedging and also suitable fencing materials. Finally there is a small
arboretum and a nature trail including Cornish wild flowers. Here
soil has been brought in from particular areas such as The Lizard.
There is a large greenhouse in which techniques of mist propaga-

tion, soil warming cables and capillary irrigation beds can be demonstrated.

In a small area such as 6½ acres is included a multitude of sound projects and Societies can apply for demonstration tours of the gardens from the County Horticultural Organiser Mr P. Blake, County Hall, Truro, TR1 3BH to whom great credit is due for having set up this useful advisory feature. A visit here will combine with a visit to the wonderful garden at Trewithen, which is adjacent.

Glendurgan

The National Trust and Mrs Fox

On the Helford River, 5 miles SW of Falmouth, and ½ mile SW of Mawnan Smith on road to Helford Passage. Garden open April– September, Mondays and Wednesdays, 10.30 am–4.30 pm, also Fridays in April and May. House not open. Garden laid out and planned by Alfred Fox early nineteenth century and planting continued by each successive generation. Given to the National Trust by Mr Cuthbert Fox and his wife in 1962 and now managed by his son Mr Philip Fox. Soil acid over shillet with some clay. Rainfall 43.3 in.

Glendurgan is a medium sized garden made in a valley which leads down to the Helford River. It has maturity and charm and from the house one has a magnificent view over the valley and from view points one can see the Helford River. It is an ever-changing kaleidoscope of varying shades of greens and purples and when the rhododendrons are in flower in April, May and June, of varying shades of pink, reds and whites.

Below the house the first plant one notices is a large *Agave americana*, which flowered in 1976, growing in the grass, while gigantic *Drimys winteri* and Chilean fire bushes, *Embothrium coccineum*, flower well at the edge of the lawn. These have reached a great size, perhaps 40 ft in height. Between them the view is dominated by a large *R. x loderi* 'King George' beside which is the grey-blue weeping Arizona cypress, *Cupressus arizonica*, not the upright form usually seen but the weeping one. Beside it is a large *Cornus capitata* which sows self-sown seedlings around. A large weeping beech, with several stems, dominates the view. It must be at least 150 years old. *Cunninghamia sinensis* is outstanding and can be seen from the house. To the left of the path one can deviate to see a large *Camellia reticulata* 'Captain Rawes' while opposite are large bushes of rhododendron 'Fragrantissimum', 'Saffron-Queen' and 'Penjerrick', one of the loveliest hybrids raised in Cornwall. There is also here an old *Acacia dealbata*, the mimosa which begins flowering in January, and other camellias of great age, 'Ville de Nantes' and 'Preston Rose'.

Proceeding down the hill one comes to a large loquat; although Mrs Fox told us that it did not fruit, the large leathery leaves are very distinct. Near the fork of the path are two very old tulip trees (*Liriodendron tulipifera*) said to be the biggest in the county, perhaps 150 years old. Their branches have become horizontal as well as vertical. Ferns grow happily along them. Everywhere as an under-cover are masses of small daffodils, the Lent lilies, followed by prim-roses and bluebells. Later there are columbines. In the valley below a little stream flows by a planting of *Primula helodoxa* with tree ferns, *Dicksonia antarctica, Magnolia x soulangiana* and *M.denudata*, a handkerchief tree, *Davidia involucrata*, which was white with handkerchiefs in 1976, and dawn redwoods *Metasequoia glypto-stroboides* and *Taxodium distichum* 'Pendulum'. Having passed some well grown *Eucryphia x intermedia*, here also is a clump of large *Eucryphia x nymansensis* 'Nymansay' which does not flower till late July and continues through August and *Magnolia campbelii* subsp. *mollicomata* and a big *M.*'Lennei' by the swamp. Higher up the valley is a large Japanese cedar, *Cryptomeria japonica*. Proceeding still down the valley is a large group of mauve and blue *Rhododendron augustinii*, mostly lighter forms while nearby are forms of the late-flowering *R.crassum*, and earlier *R.Barclayi* 'Helen Fox', a lovely red named after Barclay Fox's mother and 'Beauty of Tremough'. *Prunus* 'Tai-Haku' and 'Kanzan' provide suitable contrast, while hanging over the stream is a Cornish-raised hybrid rhododendron with large white bells. There is a deodar cedar on its island in the little pond with arum lilies around.

If one proceeds down the valley passing large drimys on the

right and tree ferns one comes to the little village of Durgan, a peaceful hamlet in spring although no longer so in August. Coming back up the other side through masses of ferns one comes to the maze made out of laurel and kept clipped. This is very old and one of the largest in the country and is a great feature of the garden. It is also unusual to find it made of laurel. Above it on the right is a large tree of *Quercus phellos* and beside it is *Michelia doltsopa*, whose rusty buds and sweet smelling white flowers are lovely in early May. It is a relation of the magnolias. Everywhere there are masses of blue hydrangeas for summer colour. Coming up to the walled garden behind the house one will find more unusual trees and shrubs, although originally intended for fruit. Here are *Clerodendron trichotomum* with its turquoise blue berries and red calyces in September and the tender *Albizzia lophantha* from Western Australia, one of the finest of foliage plants where it can be grown. Against the wall are the lobster claw from New Zealand *Clianthus puniceus, Acacia longifolia* and *A.dealbata, Cytisus battandieri* and *Pittosporum tenuifolium* 'Garnetti', the finest of the silvery white and pink leaved Pittosporum. For the summer there are great clumps of deep blue and white agapanthus and bushes of *Hypericum* 'Rowallane', 8 ft or more high. This is the best of the hypericums for a mild area. The fuchsias are left out all the year.

There are very fine copper beeches at the end of the drive as you approach the house apart from those in the valley. One notices them as one leaves carrying away a memory of much beauty in a lovely setting and many very fine trees and rhododendrons and a particular atmosphere of peace and quiet.

Ince Castle

Viscount and Viscountess Boyd

By A374 about 3 miles from Saltash, turn south at Trematon, then follow signposts. Open one Wednesday in May and one in June in aid of National Gardens Scheme, St John's Benevolent Association and local charities 2–6 pm. House not open. Garden Centre and plants for sale. A woodland and landscape garden made by present owners. Soil acid, shale. Rainfall average 28 in.

Ince Castle is a lovely mellow red brick house, built with bricks possibly imported from the Netherlands by the Killigrew family. It looks out across the water of the Tamar estuary towards Antony House. As one enters, a vast Turkey oak, over 200 years old, has fallen over the grass with horizontal branches but is still preserved with care and is well worth looking at. In the grass on the opposite side is a young *Robinia* 'Frisia' yellow in the spring, while growing from the steps opposite is an unusually large specimen of the lemon verbena (*Aloysia citriodora*). Under the wall bordering the drive is an attractive border with *Caryopteris*, *Viburnum*, grey foliaged plants and a mass of the tall blue *Echiums*, seedlings from Tresco Abbey, flowering in mid summer.

A charming paved courtyard looks out on the south side with thymes spreading freely among the cracks surrounding a fountain in the centre. There is also a large cauldron. Against the wall of the house is a *Magnolia delavayi* with its vast leathery leaves and two large old specimens of *Magnolia grandiflora*. Against the west wall is a figure of a gladiator and two delightful lead peacocks, planted with the silvery *Convolvulus cneorum* which contrasts well with the red *Leptospermums* and the tall *Lobelia tupa* from Chile with deep crimson spikes in late summer. *Feijoa sellowiana* with its mass of deep red stamens has grown into a large shrub by the wall.

On the south side is an attractive sunk garden with pebbled paths and a great variety of plants, some dwarf rhododendrons, grey foliaged cinerarias and the prickly *Fascicularia bicolor* with its bright red bracts and blue flowers in the centre of the rosettes. The bright blue berried dianellas from Tasmania are conspicuous in the autumn and contrast well with the greyish *Garrya elliptica* with its long catkins. At the end of the sunk garden is a pool with water lilies and on the side a fascinating shell house made by Lord Boyd and his family with very ornamental shells and minerals from all over the world stuck in the walls. An ostrich egg is placed in the centre of the roof. Beyond the lily pond is a mass of rugosa roses and a well disguised swimming pool behind, well shielded also against the wind.

On the east side of the house is another paved terrace with magnolias behind against the house and on the house is the lovely white moschata rose from Nepal, a selected form known as 'La Mortola'.

Low curved beds have been built into the grass of the lawn in front and behind is a ha-ha so that the view across the water is not interrupted. In the spring the grass is thick with daffodils and in the bed is a variety of foliaged shrubs and herbaceous plants. Grey foliaged ones predominate such as the white *Buddleia fallowiana*. There are also cistus, tamarix, artemisias and many hebes, which withstood well the drought of 1976. Sedum 'Ruby Glow' follows an abundance of alchemilla and yellow-leaved sage. The unusual purple-flowered shrubby pea *Lespedeza thunbergii* flowers freely in late summer and early autumn. White leptospermums with grey foliage mingle in well. A scarlet oak is becoming a valuable feature. *Helichrysum serotinum*, the curry plant, formerly and better known as *H.angustifolium*, scents the air as one brushes against it. White cattle graze beyond the ha-ha.

To the north-east side of the house is a cherry walk with a grass path beside it leading down to a woodland garden in a dell. Here are some of the finer magnolias such as *M.campbellii* well placed so that one can look across and down at them with an old bowling green in front. In the centre is an old cider press with the stones made into a cascade and surrounded by moisture loving primulas and scarlet **Lobelia fulgens. There are two charming little marble figures from** Lord Iveagh's former house in St James's Square. The larger-leaved hydrangeas such as *H.sargentiana* and *H.villosa* seem to have withstood the drought well, better than the Hortensia ones and they are also more interesting and graceful as plants. Other plants in this area include the scarlet-twigged maple *Acer* 'Senkaki', the lovely yellow berried *Sorbus* 'Joseph Rock', New Zealand flax *Phormium* *tenax* and the pink-berried *Sorbus vilmorinii* and a good Judas tree, purplish pink in spring. Rhododendrons including the large-leaved *R.sino-grande* survived the drought. This dell is protected from the south-west wind.

By the house are two interesting walled gardens, a white garden with the silver-leaved *Artemisia arborescens* and other grey-leaved plants and in the centre a statue by Gertrude Knoblock. The other is purposely designed as a contrast, a garden of warm colours, rich oranges and crimsons contrasted with grey leaves such as *Melianthus major* which I have always considered as one of the most distinguished of all grey-leaved plants. The old dahlia 'Bishop of Llandaff' with its scarlet flowers and reddish foliage still shows up better than many of the newer varieties while among them are such plants as *Beschorneria yuccoides* from Mexico with its six foot pink stems with drooping green and pink flowers. It flourishes in the sun. The pretty yellow *Crocosmia* 'Solfatare', so much pleasanter than many of the modern montbretias, grows well and red nasturtiums creep among the other plants such as the scarlet *Salvia grahamii*. Other features I particularly noticed were the very strong orange of the lion's tail *Leonotis leonurus*, *Tithonia rotundi-folia*, a very striking annual from Mexico like a tall zinnia, but rarely seen. The golden hop trailed among them. It is one of the most effective of plants. I also noticed a fine cork oak *Quercus suber* and the yellow flowered *Koelreuteria paniculata*, so valuable for its late summer flowering.

Altogether this is a garden of much variety and many choice plants. Much stress has been laid on good foliage and also on grey-leaved plants. It is a garden with something of interest throughout the year, like most well designed gardens, although the summer will naturally give the greatest colour effects. It is well worth a visit.

Lamellen

Major E.W.M. Magor and his daughter
Mrs J.D. Peter Hoblyn

Main entrance off A39 Wadebridge–Camelford road, 5 miles NE of
Wadebridge near St Tudy. Garden open several days in April and May in
aid of St John Ambulance and National Gardens Scheme, 2–6 pm;
when entrance is only by the upper drive from the direction of St Tudy.
A large garden with many rhododendrons, including hybrids, made by
Major Magor's father, Mr E.J.P. Magor. Soil acid, variable with much
leaf mould but overlying heavy clay and slate. Rainfall average 35 in.

Lamellen is in a valley sheltered except for gales from the north-
west, and is only a few miles from the Atlantic coast. There is a
wonderful view from the house over the valley. Some of the
rhododendrons have grown to a great size and so have the Irish
yews and the cryptomerias, one of which by the upper pond was
measured in 1963 by Alan Mitchell at 87 ft with a girth of 12 ft
2 in. It is one of the largest in the country. Other notable conifers
include *Cunninghamia lanceolata*, *Athrotaxis selaginoides*, a fine
Thuya plicata 'Zebrina' and a big *Podocarpus totara*. The 'Cornish
Red' rhododendrons ('Russellianum') have grown to a great size.
Most of Mr Magor's hybrids bear 'portmanteau' names made from
the first part of the two parent species' names, on the system suggested
by the late Professor Sir Isaac Bayley Balfour, Regius Professor at
Edinburgh. After Mr Magor's death in 1941 the garden became
very overgrown. Major Magor and the late Mrs Magor started
reclamation in 1962 and now most of the plants can be seen to
good effect. New planting is in progress and includes some notable
plants from Brodick and from Windsor. These include *Magnolia
sargentiana robusta* and *M.cylindrica* and a particularly good form of
Rhododendron mollyanum grown from seed from Benmore.

Coming down the drive one passes a fine group of *R.augustinii*,
showing how variable is the species. The blue-mauve flowers stand
out at a distance. Various hybrids have been made from them and
one 'St Breward' was selected in this garden from *R.augustinii* x

impeditum and later gained an FCC, the highest award given to a plant. It is an intense deep violet-mauve colour and very free-flowering. *R.*'Lamellen', a cross of *R.campanulatum* x *R.griffithianum* also originated here and in the best forms shows a peculiar upright growth with large white flowers, many in bud. The plant here is different from the one grown at Tower Court and now usually distributed as 'Lamellen', which also came from here but lacks the *campanulatum* colour. A large plant of *R.macabeanum*, probably from the original introduction, is a good form though not quite so good as those at Trewithen and Trengwainton. Along the top of both sides of the valley are some very old *Pinus radiata* originally planted as wind-break.

A group of *R.carolinianum* hybrids made at Windsor has been planted near the drive, the crosses with *sulfureum* and with *mucronulatum* being particularly good. Near it is a very nice plant of the Windsor *R.yakusimanum* growing below a *Stewartia pseudocamellia* 20 ft or so fall, which flowers in July with white flowers not unlike small single camellias and sometimes gives good autumn colour. Also notable is a clump of *R.*'Gauntletti', an old hybrid and a fine *R.neriiflorum* with its scarlet flowers which regularly flowers again in October. The original plant of *R.*'Damaris' ('Dr Stocker' x *R.campylocarpum*) which was one of the first of the yellow hybrids is still here. 'Mrs Kingsmill' raised from the same cross as 'Penjerrick' is also a good yellow, though rather paler. *Magnolia globosa* also from Windsor is growing into a large plant and above the terrace close to the house is an enormous *Magnolia campbellii* under the shelter of a north wall, and this flowers well in mid-March four years out of five. *Magnolia delavayi* has also made a large plant against this wall and under it is the rare *R.lyi*, a plant of the *Maddenii* Series. It has scented white trumpets with a yellow blotch. Another rare plant near it is *R.mollicomum* of the *Scabri-folium* Series, which has axillary pink flowers crowded near the top of the shoot. Behind the wall are other *Maddeniis*, including *R.ciliicalyx*, a beautiful species with creamy white flowers with a green base, and *scopulorum*. Here also is the hybrid *R.*'Tyermanii' (*R.formosum* x *R.nutallii*) with enormous white flowers, usually only seen as a greenhouse plant.

Most of Mr Magor's hybrids were planted in groups of three which usually show variation. *R.*'Gilian' was raised from *R. campylocarpum* x *R.griffithianum* but is red, fading to cream and is a particularly good cross named after his wife. This was one of the parents of R.'Hermione', also an Award of Merit plant, and of R.'Clio', both of which are still to be seen in the garden. There are fine old plants of *R.houlstonii* and of *R.fortunei*, grown from Wilson seed, as are the pink and the white forms of *R.calophytum*, the pink one from here forming the original for the plate in the Botanical Magazine. A fine cross of this with *R.arboreum* received an Award of Merit in 1976 and has been named 'Tretawn'. *R.irroratum* is here in a number of forms, one very speckled form being most striking. *R.magorianum*, also of the same series, was discovered here from Wilson's seed and named after Mr Magor, although unfortunately it is not now in general cultivation. There are several forms too of 'Oreocinn', one of Mr Magor's hybrids in general cultivation raised from *R.oreotrephes* and *R.cinnabarinum* which demonstrates well his use of portmanteau names. At the top of the wood is a good plant of *Acer griseum* with its stems branched near the top, showing well its peeling bark, as does *Betula albo-sinensis* nearby. *Picea smithiana* with its drooping branches was also a good specimen and a beautiful tree.

Great tribute should be paid to Major Magor and his late wife for the way in which this garden of valuable plants has been restored and for the beauty it now gives. It is always good to see new life coming back into a garden and with so much success, and it is encouraging that this work is likely to continue under the younger generation.

Lanhydrock House

The National Trust

Near Bodmin 2½ miles SE of Bodmin on B3268–Lostwithiel. Garden open November–March during daylight. 1 April–31 October, daily 11 am–1 pm and 2–6 pm, last admission at 5.30 pm. House also open. Restaurant. Large park, formal garden and woodland garden surrounding a magnificent house. Given to National Trust by Lord Clifden in 1953. Garden started about 1860 by Lord Robartes and largely replanted by seventh Lord Clifden after 1930 with flowering trees and shrubs and subsequently by the National Trust. Soil acid overlying clay. Rainfall, average.

Lanhydrock is approached by one of the most magnificent avenues in the country, formerly of sycamores but now mainly of mature beeches which have been used to replace the sycamore as they fell. It is beautiful in spring when the young foliage appears, and again in autumn. Passing through the Gothic style gate house one enters the formal garden with upright yews well trimmed and cut flat at the top. They are very old but still seem to be in perfect condition. Among them are some unusually fine urns brought from Bagatelle, just outside Paris. Beds of hybrid tea and floribunda roses are planted also in spring with bedding plants and edged with box. On the wall of the courtyard are ancient *Magnolia grandiflora*, trimmed nearly to the wall and flowering for much of the summer, and on each side of the main door are two very large trimmed camellias (*C.japonica* 'Adolphe Audusson') with bright crimson flowers in March and April. These are splendidly maintained. Around the walls have also been planted various shrubby ever-green hebes (veronicas), kept clipped to about 3 ft some less. The foliage varies in colour and is decorative throughout the year, but especially when young, and complements well the grey granite of the walls as well as being largely labour-saving. This is a clever piece of planting which could well be copied more widely.

Lanhydrock has a large collection of both mature and young magnolias which well merit visits both during March (for the *campbellii-mollicomata* group) and during April for the *veitchii* and the *soulangiana* group. To see these and the upper woodland garden on the hillsides behind the house, turn right by a small path at the edge of the house and after going through part of the formal garden and then by a small gate turn left up the hill. The first magnolia is a large 50 ft tree of *M.kobus* covered with white flowers in April. Beyond it is a promising young specimen of the pink-flowered hybrid 'Leonard Messel' raised at Nymans in Sussex and rapidly becoming not only one of the most beautiful but also most popular magnolias. It is a hybrid between *M.stellata rosea* and *M.kobus*. Here also are old trees of some of the early *Rhododendron arboreum* hybrids such as 'Cornish Red', now 30 or 40 ft tall. Later there are other colourful hybrids such as the rather strident deep purplish pink 'Cynthia', the deeper red 'Mars' and the large-flowered 'Loderi' forms with enormous trusses of white or pale blush pink flowers, giving their effect from their great size. For later colour there are also hydrangeas and kalmias, the American mountain laurels. In April two large trees of the white form of *Magnolia* x *veitchii* 'Isca', perhaps 60 ft tall and covered with upright flowers are very impressive and one gets good views of them from further up the hill with the house and parkland behind. These are hybrids of *M.campbellii* x *M.denudata*. A large tree of *M.campbellii* behind is 40–50 ft tall but the flowers in March are more susceptible to frosts. It was good to see that the National Trust had planted close a good young specimen tree of the white form of *M.campbellii*, by many regarded as even more beautiful than the pink form, also *M.dawsoniana*. A little stream runs down the hillside and tends to keep the soil damper. I also saw large trees of *M.sargentiana robusta* another of the large-flowered early species and also of the later flowering *M.hypoleuca* with large and most decorative leaves. Another species of the same group but even more tender and with even larger leaves was *M.rostrata*, of which a young tree seemed to be doing well. Lanhydrock will continue as one of the interesting magnolia gardens of Cornwall and they have a splendid setting. I noticed near the wall at the top of the garden a healthy young tree of the tender *Michelia doltsopa*, a close relation of the magnolias which has furry rusty brown buds and heavily scented creamy white flowers in late April and May.

If one climbs a little further and turns to the left one comes to an unusual feature, a magnolia arch made from *M.soulangiana* 'Lennei' where the rather loose growing young branches have been tied down to a metal arch. It flowers freely in April and I thought was effective in this sloping setting. Further on are large trees of two good cornus *C.nuttalii* from Western America flowering in late April and *C.kousa* from China. Interesting young maples have been planted among the older trees of Japanese maples. Throughout the garden there are many old bushes of camellias, both *C.japonica*, *C.x williamsii* and *C.reticulata* some of which have reached a great size and give masses of early colour over a long season. 'Captain Rawes', the semi-double form of *C.reticulata* was a splendid sight covering the wall of a small cottage near the top of the garden.

If, instead of turning left near there, one goes to the right behind a semi-circle of clipped yew, a new herbaceous garden has been planted by the National Trust with interesting plants, paeonies, yuccas, agapanthus, veratrum, kniphofias and hemerocallis. In the spring the apple green flowered *Helleborus corsicus* was striking. This is such a good garden plant both in flower and foliage.

In its setting of magnificent old beeches this will always be a beautiful park to visit and enjoy and is now being well cared for by the National Trust.

Pencarrow

The Molesworth-St Aubyn Family

4 miles NW of Bodmin off A389 and B266 near Washaway. Garden open mid April–end June. Sunday and Wednesday 1 July–3 October. Wednesday, Thursday and Sunday, also Easter Saturday and Monday, Spring and Summer Bank holidays, 1.45–5.30 pm. House also open. A formal garden near house and large woodland garden with old collection of trees, especially mature conifers. Made by ancestors of present family. Soil acid, heavy loam. Rainfall high.

Pencarrow has been in possession of the Molesworth family since Elizabethan times. It lies in a secluded valley between Bodmin and Wadebridge in North Cornwall and only a few miles from the north coast and is approached by a mile of drive. Along the drive is a well wooded area with many of the specimen conifers for which Pencarrow is noted. These were planted mainly by Sir William Molesworth, Bt, who was an MP from 1831 onwards. This was the time of the great collectors in America and the introduction of the vast range of conifers by the Royal Horticultural Society and through the great firm of Veitch of Exeter. It was a favourable site for these and they grew well but by now many are over-mature and have lost their leaders or died. Seed came from Douglas, the greatest of all the collectors in America and later from William Lobb, a Cornishman working for Veitch. More seed, particularly of rhododendrons, came from Sir Joseph Hooker, collected by him in the Himalayas about 1850, from Wallich, the famous director of the Calcutta gardens, and from Sir William's brother Francis from New Zealand. Sir William was one of the earlier gardeners to go out into the woods to find space for his seedlings. All these have been mapped carefully by Lt Col J.A. Molesworth-St Aubyn and divided into lettered areas. Many have been measured by Alan Mitchell of the Forestry Commission. The visitor anxious to see the best trees should consult his guide on The Trees of Pencarrow which is available at the house.

He will probably start from the house and look first at the formal Italian garden in front of the house, now much simplified. In the centre of a large green sunken area towards the south of the house is an ornamental fountain with a lily pool around and on each side of it are domed cypresses. Along the house there are beds of bearded irises and floribunda roses making colour in the summer. On the house are large wisterias and *Magnolia grandiflora* which is kept low off the fine architecture of the house and a white climbing *Rosa bracteata* which was still flowering in September. This was introduced from China by Lord Macartney's mission in 1793 and is still known as the Macartney rose. Behind the house near the tearoom and services area is one of the finest specimens of the deep pink *Magnolia campbellii* that I have seen, clothed, to the ground and open to a lawn at one side it must be 70 or 80 ft high and in the late summer was covered with bud. Pencarrow, however, is rather a frost pocket at the foot of its valley and in more years than otherwise we were told it was spoilt by spring frost. A wall with climbing roses and other shrubs stretches from near the front door and protects a lawn on which are some interesting cultivars of *Chamaecyparis obtusa*, the Hinoki cypress of Japan, a very large *Pinus radiata* and several *Nothofagus obliqua*, the Robel beech from Chile, planted in 1906 and now a good size. By the house are two fine cedars, a deodar of 65 ft planted in 1848 and *C.atlantica* and a cedar of Lebanon by the Rockery. *Calocedrus decurrens* the upright incense cedar from California makes a tall spire near the house. Then behind are some very tall beeches by the old drive which form a good background. As one walks past an enormous *Cotoneaster frigidus* grown almost into a spreading tree and enters the area of an old rockery made out of great blocks of stone carried from Bodmir Moor by carts, but now overgrown with evergreen azaleas, there are rhododendrons and large maples, a fine sight both in early summer and in autumn. Beside it are fine specimens of *Juniperus chinensis*, a tree with many varieties, and the graceful drooping *Juniperus·recurva* now over 36 ft. I also noted a fine *Cunninghamia lanceolata* with its broad leaflets, although nearly always its effect is spoilt by some of the older branches dying back behind the green shoot at the end. However it is a handsome tree which always attracts attention. Unusual also are the 'Cristata' form of *Cryptomeria japonica*, with its flattened cockscomb branchlets aggregated into a small dome, and nearly the oldest known *Taxodium ascendens* 'Nutans', the pond cypress, and a *Metasequoia glyptostroboides*, the dawn redwood, both a fresh green. As one crosses the grass meadow which has been cleared one comes to some unusually fine *Cupressus macrocarpa* with spreading branches. Paths have been cleared through the woodland and one can now walk along the area of the old Palm House, now no longer functional, to the lake and the area known as the American gardens from the numerous American conifers planted there. By the lake there is a fine *Davidia involucrata* with its hanging white pocket handkerchiefs in spring, a fine *Rhododendron falconeri* and an enormous *Magnolia soulangiana* with others nearby. Next to the *Davidia* are *Podocarpus nubigenus* and *P. salignus*, the willow-leaved podocarp, both from Chile and both well over 30 ft tall. They form elegant small trees or large bushes, not unlike yews but with longer leaflets.

Near the lake also are two large wing-nuts, *Pterocarya fraxinifolia* from the Caucasus and *P. stenoptera* from China. They make very handsome trees with long racemes of pendulous green flowers. Another *Cunninghamia*, notable for its huge bole and trunk, was measured by Alan Mitchell as nearly 80 ft. In the American garden is an old *Pinus montezumae* of 22 ft, which Mitchell has recorded as the tallest now known of this very handsome grey long-needled conifer from Mexico.

One can now either cross the field or go round at the end of it to the main drive along which are many very old conifers and rhododendrons. The latter have been largely planted by Sir John Molesworth-St Aubyn, the present baronet and have been his particular interest over the years. I noticed a large *R. macabeanum* close to the weeping *Picea brewerana*, one of the most lovely of all conifers and planted at the rear of the drive by the late Sir Hugh

Molesworth-St Aubyn in 1928, rather later than some of the biggest spruces which date from the 1840s. Particularly tall are the tiger-tail spruce at 80 ft but with the largest bole known and the lovely weeping *Pinus smithiana* at 90 ft, a beautiful tree in good health. The silver firs, *Abies alba, A.homolepis* from Japan, *A.procera* the noble fir from Western North America, are all worth pausing for and some are still bearing their handsome upright cones. There are several good specimens of *Cryptomeria japonica* which have made very handsome trees. Among the pines is an unusual fine specimen of *P.armandii.* the white pine from China, originally collected by the White Father Père Armand David and fittingly named after him since it is one of the most handsome of all pines with its long bluish green cones. One of the features of Pencarrow is the remains of the great avenue of monkey puzzles *Araucaria araucana* for which one has to follow the drive across the road to the opposite side of the main entrance gate. The largest is 72 ft in height. They were probably planted from William Lobb's collected seed in Chile in 1844.

Pencarrow is a rewarding garden for those who will take the trouble to search through the undergrowth with the guide to the trees but allow several hours in which to find the best. It is good that care is now being taken to recover some of it from the war years.

Penjerrick

Mrs J.M.K. Fox

1 mile S of Budock Water. Garden open Wednesdays and Sundays 2–4.30 pm. House not open. Large garden made by Fox family, who came to Cornwall in 1749. Beeches planted in early 1800s. Soil acid, warm and sheltered garden.

Penjerrick is the garden where some of the most famous of the Cornish rhododendrons were raised. 'Cornish Cross' (*griffithianum* x *thomsonii*), 'Penjerrick' (*griffithianum* x *campylocarpum* var *elatum*), cream, white and pink forms, and many others were raised by Mr S. Smith the head gardener. It is still a lovely garden dominated by large copper beeches and other trees, although in later years a lack of labour has left some of the trees lying where they fell.

A large glade stretches away from the house to a fence where a path under a great copper beech tree leads by an ornamental wooden bridge across the road. A very good *Rhododendron augustinii* catches the eye. From the top of the glade one looks out at another large copper beech with below it a large *Magnolia delavayi*, one of the largest I have ever seen. Its leaves are still large and it seems in perfect health. Behind it was one of the most enormous *Eucryphia cordifolia* that I have ever seen; it must have made a wonderful sight in flower in early August. It was at least 80–90 years old. A *Magnolia campbellii* leans over the lawn and behind it a great *embothrium*, a mass of flaming orange-red in early May. Under the shade of a large copper beech are primroses and bluebells and a double white *Saxifraga grandiflora*, growing in the lawn. An Italian cypress, an upright exclamation mark breaks the spreading branches in front of a large monkey puzzle, perhaps one of the original trees. On the right at the top of the glade were vast Irish yews and below large groups of *Rhododendron* 'Hinodegiri' and 'Hinomayo', though wisely kept separate. These were backed by **Camellia japonica 'Alba Plena' and Myrtus lechlerana with white** flowers like pearls in spring contrasting well with the dark green foliage. *Magnolia sargentiana* and a vast *M. hypoleuca* flowering well dominated the back of the glade. *Pieris forrestii* was dripping white trusses of flower among scarlet leaves. On the left of the lawn at the end were fine masses of rhododendron 'Lady Alice Fitzwilliam' 20 ft across and 8 ft tall, billowing with flower. Beside it was the kurume azalea 'Apple Blossom', more *R. augustinii* and *R. davidsonianum* and *R. cinnabarinum* var. *roylei*, beside a superb cut-leaved beech and an even more superb *Davidia involucrata* near the road, with many trunks over 50 ft tall and literally dripping with handkerchiefs. It was a lovely sight. Then we came to the cream 'Penjerrick' rhododendron, 20 ft tall and covered with flower, the creamy bells so beautifully shaped and hanging loosely on the red petioles. This received its award in 1943. Beside it was more 'Lady Alice Fitzwilliam', *R. vaseyi*, and behind a large *Eucryphia moorei*. Billowing masses of *R.* x 'Loderi', 'King George' and 'Loderi Pink Diamond' were beside a big *Paulownia* at least 40 years old. A large rhododendron 'Cornish Cross', must have been one of the original plants of Mr Smith who retired in 1935. A huge evergreen *P.salignus* was 40 ft tall at least and layered all round and so we came back to the top of the glade.

For those willing to persevere across the bridge there were more rewards, a lovely weeping beech with underneath it tree fern seedlings nestling among wood sorrel on the trunk of a tree fern. Beside it was the lovely copper beech already referred to. Then one came to the water garden, rather overgrown but with some fine rhododendrons, *R.sinogrande* and *R.giganteum* flowering in February, tree ferns and gunneras, *Magnolia sargentiana* and a group of *M.stellata*.

So we completed our tour of this magical and romantic garden where there are many more fine plants to be found.

St Michael's Mount

The National Trust and The Hon J.F. St Aubyn

From Marazion by causeway at low tide or by boat, about 3 miles E of Penzance by A394. Open throughout year. Monday, Wednesday and Friday 9.30 am–7 pm May–September but closing earlier in other months, and 1 November–31 March by guided tours only. House open also. A unique garden made on a steep rocky island with practically no frost but susceptible to salt spray. Soil acid above granite. Rainfall about 28 in.

St Michael's Mount is an unusual site on a small island off Marazion in Mount's Bay a few miles east of Penzance. The Castle is a most dramatic building standing 250 ft up on solid rock. The garden has been built among the rocks around it, exposed mostly to wind and sea spray. Sheltered pockets and sites have been made and it is practically frost free, a most challenging site, and great use of it has been made by Lord St Levan and his son, Mr John St Aubyn, who now lives in the Castle. The gardens cling to the hillside as one imagines the hanging gardens of Babylon may have done. It is like one gigantic rock garden. The rock is granite, vast grey boulders, and the soil is acid, mostly thin and composed of the disintegrating rock. The annual rainfall usually averages about 28 in., but was much less in 1976 as elsewhere in the country.

One crosses from Marazion by the causeway if it is open, if not by boat ferry, and then climbs up towards the castle. The gardens lie below the castle and one walks round the eastern side, the most sheltered, by a wide grass path. Some groups of *Pinus radiata* have been planted and provide some shelter, but they are windswept and need to be continually reinforced by more planting. The gardener told me that the foresters from the mainland prefer to plant in the spring in April and May rather than in the autumn. Kniphofias and agapanthus are everywhere and have naturalised among the bracken and grass and in groups against the rocks. They provide fine colour in August and early September. The agapanthus have grown very large with massive heads. Among the kniphofias I noticed the late flowering but very handsome *K.roopiae* with large heads of yellow and red. On the rocks are masses of mesembryanthe-mums of various sorts but mostly the large *Carpobrotus edulis*, the Hottentot fig which has been naturalised in various parts of Cornwall around the coast. On the rocks are great bosses, some-times yards across, of the prickly *Fascicularia bicolor* from Chile which has tight clusters of blue flowers in the centre of the rosette surrounded by bright red bracts, a most unusual and striking plant but tender in many gardens. This used to be known as *Rhodostachys bicolor*. Masses of polyanthus narcissi, some of the form known as The mount lily and also double trumpet daffodils have become naturalised and make a lovely sight in spring. The yellow Spanish broom (*Spartium junceum* also grows well and *Rosa rugosa* seems to stand the wind and the sprays, so do the large bulbs of *Amaryllis belladonna* which flower in autumn with the agapanthus. There is a small walled garden let into the rock and facing south which has more protection and some interesting plants, *Myrtus luma* (*M.apiculata*) with lovely bark and flowering in summer, the orange *Leonotis leonurus*, the lion's tail, with shoots up to 5 or 6 ft tall and clusters up the stem of very bright orange flowers in late summer and early autumn. It is usually regarded as a tender plant, only for very sheltered hot sites. There was also the tender orange *Cassia corymbosa* and *Jasminum polyanthum*, so sweet smelling and the uncommon little hybrid *Correa harrisii* with pendulous pink trumpet like bells. On the wall the *Feijoa sellowiana* grew and flowered well. It belongs to the myrtle family and has conspicuous masses of red stamens in the centre of the flower and later edible fruit. It comes from Brazil. Here also was the brilliant red *Erythrina crista-galli* which flowers in late summer, the flowers looking like small shields well burnished and shining. The daturas grew well and there were forms with orange flowers and abutilons such as 'Canary Bird' with hanging yellow bells. White arum lilies and cinerarias grew well and spread. The mauve *Convolvulus mauretanicus* hung in mats from the rocks and was a good plant for this area. It was most unusual to see the Guernsey lily *Nerine sarniensis* growing well outside and throwing up flower spikes. This is much more tender than the pink *Nerine bowdenii* and is usually grown as a greenhouse plant. It has many different coloured forms. There were also watsonias, like brightly coloured gladioli, the yellow *Calceolaria integrifolia* which lasts the winter outside here. Pelargoniums of various sorts grew against the rocks while the orange-red *Campsis* climbed against the rocks. Olearias also seemed to survive the wind well.

On the north side of the island, which is more protected, one walked up through a small wood of pines and sycamores and here are hydrangeas and griselinias and many camellias and yellow azaleas. In the middle of a Cornish cross of cobbles and stone in the ground is the beautiful pink *Camellia* x *williamsii* 'Donation' one of the most free-flowering varieties in the genus. An unusual triumph is a plant of *Lapageria rosea* climbing up into a sycamore and we were told that it produced many beautiful crimson bells. A Judas tree *Cercis siliquastrum* is another feature and there are a number of rhododendrons which survive the wind.

St Michael's Mount is a garden of dramatic possibilities for plants which will survive the wind and sprays and it is surprising how many of these there are. It is well worth a visit at different seasons.

Trelissick

The National Trust

4 miles S of Truro, off A39 Truro–Falmouth. Turn left signposted on B3289 to King Harry Passage. Garden open March–October. Weekdays 11 am–6 pm, Sundays 2–6 pm. House not open. Garden shop near entrance. Large tree and shrub garden planted by Mr Ronald and Mrs Copeland. Given to National Trust by Mr Copeland in 1935 and continued by the National Trust. Many of the flowers painted on Copeland China were grown here. Soil acid, shillet overlying clay. Rainfall average for area, 41 in.

On the left it is well worth entering the small 'Parsley Garden' since here is no longer parsley but some unusual and tender plants. Here is *Hesperoyucca whipplei* from California, the finest of all the yuccas but with spine-like leaves. Also notable here are *Abutilon* x *suntense*, a comparatively modern hybrid, a good white *Abutilon vitifolium*, *Vestia lyciodes* dripping with yellow tubelike flowers and 8 ft × 8 ft, *Teucrium fruticans* and yellow *Grevillea sulphurea*, *Corokia macrocarpa*, *Azara microphylla* 'Variegata' and *Abutilon* 'Orange Glow', *Fabiana imbricata* and the tender *Prostanthera rotundifolia*, while there are large clumps of *Scilla liliohyacinthus*. On the wall outside is *Rosa braceata* from China, the Macartney rose flowering in June. There is a fine wisteria on the right with *Hebe fairchildi* below. By the entrance to the stable yard behind the house is a fine *Mahonia lomariifolia* and *Camellia japonica* 'Alba Plena'.

One passes through a little white gate beside a vast mass of the bright reddish-magenta azalea 'Hinodigiri', one of the best of the evergreen azaleas. On the right is the unusual *Hydrangea quercifolia*, then one wanders down the lawn past a large *Cryptomeria japonica*, the Japanese incense cedar, 40 ft high. The beds are largely planted with summer flowering plants, *Crinum* x *powellii*, fuchsias, *Melianthus major*, that most beautiful foliage plant, *Ceanothus* 'Indigo' and rose 'Golden Wings'. On the right is a large *Michelia doltsopa*, while at the bottom is *Acer pseudoplatanus* 'Brilliantissimum', shrimp-pink in spring and *Acer japonicum* 'Osakazuki', safest and most brilliant in colour of the maples. *Olearia gunniana* and *Cerato-stigma willmottianum* are lovely in spring and autumn respectively. In the autumn *Rhus trichocarpa* glowed brilliantly while *Hebe veitchii* was still a deep blue.

On retracing to the top of the grass one turns left and then by the ochre-coloured trunk of a big *Myrtus luma* (*apiculata*) one descends a dell with tree ferns and a good deep blue *Rhododendron augustinii*. On the right is a very fine form of that tender *Maddenii, R.polyandrum* with blush pink large waxy, scented flowers. Here are also bananas *Musa basjoo*, a fine red hybrid rhododendron and further on a large Oriental plane with anemones and bluebells below, *Rhododendron* 'Penjerrick Cream' and a good *Viburnum plicatum tomentosum*. This path leads on to a woodland walk and nature trail down to the beach.

Trelissick is renowned for its hydrangeas which can be seen best on the Hydrangea Walk and around the upper lawns. They are lovely in August and September.

Resuming the main path turn right over the bridge into the new plantation of Cardadden. Here are some vast *Cupressus macrocarpa, Pinus radiata* and a fine deodar cedar, but there are also young plantations and interesting plants such as *Pinus patula*, *Magnolia globosa, Pittosporum tenuifolium* 'Garnettii' whose leaves are variegated with silver and pink, and *Photinia fraseri* 'Birmingham' which some think as the finest of the red leaved photinias. On the return towards the house there are *Halesia carolina*, a fine old rhododendron 'Lady Chamberlain' and on the upper lawn I also noted a fine *Picea smithiana* and rhododendron 'Penjerrick White'. On the wall was a good *Wisteria floribunda* 'Macrobotrys' with its long racemes of flower.

Tremeer

Mrs J.H. Hopwood

Near St Tudy, 8 miles N of Bodmin by A389 and B32666. Garden open every Sunday from 28 March–6 June, 2–6 pm in aid of National Gardens Scheme. House not open. A medium-sized garden of 6 acres made in the last 25 years by General Harrison, who specialises particularly in camellias and rhododendrons. Soil acid, rainfall high, average 45 in.

Tremeer is a camellia and rhododendron enthusiasts' garden and from it have come many of the finest new hybrids shown at the Royal Horticultural Society in recent years. It also has, however, a good selection of other shrubs. Facing south and only a few miles from the Atlantic coast it is, however, a cold garden by Cornish standards and exposed to strong winds. Every bit of space has been used to full advantage and in spring and early summer it is a garden of much flower and colour. General Harrison married the late Mrs Roza Stevenson from Tower Court, near Ascot and she brought a number of very fine rhododendrons with her to an already packed garden. She was a great enthusiast for rhododendron species and raised many from collectors' seeds. She also brought with her a collection of the evergreen azaleas, made by Dr E.H. Wilson from Japan. These are infinitely variable there. When Wilson said he had the fifty best kurumes from Japan, Yokohama Nurseries said far from that we will produce a hundred that are better, and sent the hundred to Tower Court. General Harrison could only find space for fifty of the originals which presumably arrived between the wars, and a special bed was dug in the lawn in front of the house for them. They flower freely in spite of becoming covered with grey lichen and present a great mass of colour. A short drive leads up to the house. On the way one notices a floriferous *Ceanothus arboreus* 'Trewithen Blue' covered with its powder-blue flowers.

Behind the house a new plantation of camellia varieties has been made above a steep bank of dwarf rhododendrons and heathers. *R.impeditum* with its violet mauve flowers is particularly good and a compact tussock and so also are specially dark forms of *R.saluenense* and *R.russatum*. They have made a close bank completely covering the ground. The *williamsii* hybrids of Camellia are kept separate from the *japonicas* on the right. Among the *williamsii* I particularly liked 'Margaret Waterhouse', a blush pink, 'Brigadoon', in which General Harrison thinks he has a better flower than 'Donation', and 'Debbie', an American raised double pink. 'Henry Turnbull' was a good white semi-double *japonica*.

General Harrison has found that the camellias particularly the *reticulata* hybrids flower better at Tremeer in full sun than in semi-shade but in some shade the foliage is darker and better. In this plantation behind the house one should also look at some of the rhododendrons. 'Robert Keir', named after the head gardener at Tower Court, a hybrid between *R.lacteum* and *R.*'Luscombi', is a pale yellow but a flower of great substance. *R* 'Conyan' is a nice apricot fading into pink raised from *R.concatenans* and *R.concinnum* var. *pseudoyanthinum* at Tower Court, while *R.*'Arnia' is another good *concatenans* hybrid. *R.*'Edmondi' was an exceptional blood red, raised from *R.arboreum* x *R.barbatum*. One should also pause and look at a very fine *R.yakusimanum* with a large truss of flower and at the top of the steps a very good *R.russatum*, thought to be the finest in Cornwall, 6 ft x 6 ft and a very deep violet in colour.

From the terrace below the house one looks across the lawn to the rhododendrons and they show well General Harrison's interest in the violet-blues raised from *R.impeditum* and *R.augustinii*. These started with 'St Breward', selected from the neighbouring Lamellen garden, then were followed by 'St Tudy' and the latest is 'St Minver', an intense violet-blue and very floriferous. Its parents were *R.russatum* x 'St Breward'. I have not seen anywhere else such a mass of violet blue. 'Blue Star' was derived from *R.impeditum* x 'St Tudy' and is another outstanding dwarf plant of the same group. 'St Merryan' is *impeditum* x 'St Breward' and is the deepest violet blue and has recently received an Award of Merit. Along the front row is also 'Yum Yum', a delightful form of the rarely seen *R. tsariense* with blush pink flowers and a dense fawn indumentum below the leaves.

General Harrison has raised a number of hybrids from *R. williamsianum* and they are all moderate growers with delightful bell-shaped flowers produced in large numbers. My favourite is probably 'Pink Pebble' with *R.callimorphum* as its other parent.

Slightly deeper pink than its parents it is now $4\frac{1}{2}$ ft high × 7 ft across, a solid dome of colour. Others are 'Pensive' with *R.irroratum*, 'Mystic' and 'Maestro' with *R.*'Barclayi', 'Pipaluk' with *R.*'Dr Stocker'.

There are some very good yellow also. I particularly liked 'John Barr Stevenson', named after the late owner of Tower Court and also *lacteum* x 'Damaris-Logan'; of the same parentage is also 'Beatrice' which recently received an Award of Merit. 'Roza Stevenson' from **'Loderi Sir Edmund'** x *R.wardii* **is a plant which received an FCC in 1968.** The original plant of 'Damaris Logan' from Tower Court is also here, a lovely yellow and covered with flower, about 7 ft high and as much through now. It was the parent of many of his new hybrids. From Exbury he has the fine hybrid 'Mariloo', a paler yellow, 'Fortune' and 'Lionel's Triumph'. The large-leaved rhododendrons are also good, a particularly deep pink form of *R.mollyanum*, *R.sinogrande*, *R.rex* and *R.macabeanum* and a large *R.hodgsoni* of 8 ft, though there is some doubt whether it may be a hybrid.

All the paths through the rhododendrons lead down to a delightful pond at the base of the garden and one has a charming view back to the house across it, surrounded by ferns and other water loving plants. *Hydrangea petiolaris* has climed a tree. Here is 'Belle of Tremeer', a pale mauve hybrid of *R.augustinii* x *R.caeruleum album* grown into a tall plant like an *augustinii* but a clear pale silvery mauve, one of the nicest plants in this garden of beauties. In contrast *R.*'Barclayi' is enormous 20 ft × 15 ft and a brilliant scarlet and very conspicuous. It was raised by Mr Barclay Fox of Penjerrick. A good scarlet of General Harrison's raising is 'Zyxya', raised from crossing 'Barclayi' with 'Elizabeth'. Another very good red comes from 'Matador' x 'Gaul' and yet another 'Red Fortunei' x 'Laura Aberconway', as yet unnamed. Large bushes of the hybrids 'Alison Johnstone' from Trewithen and 'Peace' from Bodnant are very floriferous and make a splendid show when in flower, the pastel shades making a contrast to the scarlets.

Camellia 'Donation' is one of the star plants of the garden about 15 ft tall and absolutely dripping with pink flowers and is continually in flower from January to the beginning of May. The largest has been placed where two paths meet but in all there are fifteen in the garden. Nor should we omit a group of camellias at the east end of the garden, 'Else Jury', now 8 ft tall, 'Anticipation' from New Zealand and 'Francis L' a *reticulata* hybrid from America and among the best of the newer ones.

A large *Magnolia* x *veitchii* gives early colour in April and flowers well when frosts permit. So does the early hybrid *R.edgeworthii* x *moupinense* which has pale blush pink flowers and is scented. As one returns along the front of the house notice the fine *Pachystegia insignis* in the border, also the white *Abutilon vitifolium*, while growing up the house it is unusual to see a large *Euonymus fortunei* 'Variegatum' with yellow blotched leaves. For summer effect there are numerous eucryphias in five different varieties, and some thirty to forty different kinds of hydrangeas. Although Cornwall does not produce good autumn colour the various acers, *Parrotia persica* and *Sorbus matsumurana* from Japan usually provide a bright autumn show. An *Acer griseum* with a good trunk colours to a russet yellow.

Trengwainton

The National Trust and Major S. Bolitho

At Madron, near Heamoor on B3312 2 milesW of Penzance, from A30 turn right, signposted, just before entering Penzance, or through town, leaving by B3312 for Morvah, signposted. Open Wednesdays, Thursdays, Fridays, Saturdays 11 am–6 pm, also Bank Holiday Mondays, March–end October. See National Trust Opening Arrangements. House not open. Garden created by the late Lt Col Sir Edward Bolitho, *VMH*, and presented by him to the National Trust in 1961. Now managed by his son Major Simon Bolitho, who is also a keen and skilled gardener, with help of Gardens Adviser of the National Trust. About 250–400 feet above sea level with average annual rainfall 46 in. Usually free of severe frosts. Soil acid, loamy, over clay and granitic rock, with considerable layers of leaf mould.

Trengwainton known locally as 'the house of the springs' is indeed a garden for all seasons from March to November and one of the most favoured for tender plants in the country. Full advantage has

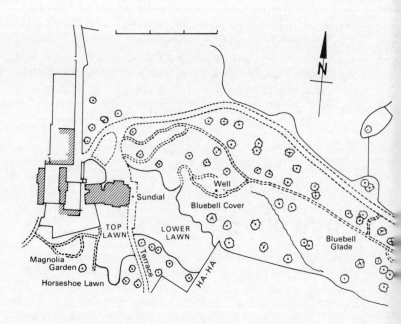

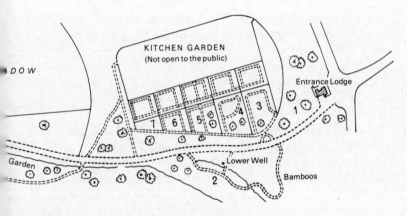

TRENGWAINTON

KITCHEN GARDEN
(Not open to the public)

DOW

Entrance Lodge

7 6 5 4 3

1

Garden

Lower Well

2

Bamboos

The numbers are referred to in the text.

been taken of this and it is an absolute treasure house of mature and rare plants as well as being a garden of beauty. It is well worth a first visit in early March when numerous rhododendron and magnolias will be in flower. The garden is a large one and if possible a couple of hours should be allowed for a thorough visit. Many of the finest rhododendron species were raised from seed from Kingdon Ward's 1927–28 expedition to North East Assam and the Mishmi Hills of Upper Burma and from this came the magnificent plants of the yellow *R.macabeanum*, one of which won an FCC, the highest award to a plant given by the Royal Horticultural Society.

One starts by the lodge at the foot of the drive and walks, slowly indeed, up the drive since many of the best plants are situated there. We will start with the right side. Near the entrance are large groups of evergreen azaleas *R.obtusum* 'Amoenum', very striking in flower colour and the white *R.mucronatum*. They are at their best in early May. Near by is a group of the later flowering deep red rhododendron 'Morvah' one of the finest hybrids raised at Trengwainton from *R.elliottii* and *R.wattii*, also an FCC plant but too tender for cold gardens. Nearby is a good form of the large-leaved *R.arizelum*.

On the right of the drive are a series of walled compartments (1 on map), interconnecting and numbered 3–7 on the map and entered by a short path and a gate. It is well worth deviating here for they contain many of the most tender and choice plants of the garden, some of which have reached a record size for this country. In the first one (no. 3) near the gate is a very large *Magnolia* x *veitchii*, a hybrid of *M.campbellii* x *M.denudata*, which flowers rather later than *M.campbellii*. It was planted in 1936. Behind it is a large *Metasequoia glyptostroboides*, the dawn redwood from China and one of the original trees to be planted in this country. It gives a lovely pinkish-terracotta autumn colouring. Here also is a very large *Embothrium coccineum* 'Norquinco Valley', probably the finest form of the Chilean fire bush and flaming with spikes of brilliant orange-red in late May and early June. About the same time one should look at the tree of magnolia 'Charles Coates', a hybrid raised at Kew from *M.sieboldii* x *M.tripetala* with creamy white scented flowers among the foliage. In this area also is a large *Eucalyptus gunnii* and in the corner by the wall a tall *Azara dentata*, a tender Chilean bush with masses of little yellow flowers made up of the stamens and smelling of chocolates in summer.

In mid March it is worth noting here *Clematis indivisa*, a tender climber from New Zealand and usually grown as a greenhouse plant, but here flowering freely outside with large white blooms. Also in flower then is the unusual Himalayan *Vaccinium retusum* with pink flowers and here several feet high. A large bush of the white *Leptospermum scoparium* flowering in May and June is against the wall and worth looking at also is a tall tree of the Tasmanian *Eucryphia milliganii*, often regarded as a variety of *E.lucida*, and covered in small white flowers in June and July. In the second walled garden (no. 4 on map) there is a large *Magnolia campbellii* flowering in late February or March and so susceptible in flower to any frosts. More uncommon in the same area is the much deeper purplish-crimson *Magnolia campbellii mollicomata* 'Lanarth', a most magnificent flower of great size and richness of colour. It was raised from the tree at Lanarth, near the Lizard, the finest of the three seedlings raised from this number of George Forrest's collecting in 1924 on the Salween-Kiu-chiang divide in Western China. It usually flowers in March a little later than the *M.campbellii*. Also starting to flower in March is the evergreen *Michelia compressa*, sometimes confused with *M.excelsa*, a name which should be considered as a synonym of the later flowering *M.doltsopa* which is also in this garden and a more lovely plant with rusty furry buds and large creamy-white scented flowers. Both are evergreens and tender. In July and August *Eucryphia moorei* from New South Wales will be covered with small, but beautifully formed white flowers, while against the wall is the tender *Abutilon globosum* 'Canary Bird', usually only seen in this country as a greenhouse plant, with large bright yellow bells over a long summer season. Also summer-flowering is a large bush of *Stewartia sinensis*, with flowers not unlike large single white roses and usually good crimson autumn colour. It also has attractive flaking bark. Also notable here is *Schima argentea*, an evergreen tree from China with white flowers in summer. This was planted in 1936.

In the next garden (5 on map) near the entrance is a tall *Styrax japonica*, planted so that one can look up at its little white bells in June and beyond are two very fine magnolias, *M.campbellii mollicomata*, a good form and the very lovely *M.sprengeri diva* which in March is often covered with bright pink chalices, 5 in. or so across and rivalling *M.campbellii* in effect and beauty. By the wall at the end of the garden is the tender *Acacia melanoxylon*, the black-wood tree from Tasmania and South Australia also flowering in March. I also noticed here the rare and tender *Malaleuca hypericifolia* from South East Australia with bright red flowers in summer. Opposite the blackwood is *Magnolia* x *watsonii*. Its creamy flowers in June have probably the strongest scent of any magnolia. It is thought to be a hybrid of *M.hypoleuca* x *M.sieboldii* and first appeared in the Japanese exhibit at the Paris exhibition of 1889. *Magnolia cylindrica*, a young tree of the more recently introduced Chinese magnolia will be found by the very large evergreen *Eucryphia cordifolia*. It has upright white flowers in April, rather like those of *M.denudata* but it is regarded by some as even preferable to this.

Here are another *Michelia doltosopa* and the very tender *Magnolia nitida* with shiny foliage. Against the walls are some tender rhododendrons, such as the bright golden yellow and early-flowering *R.chrysodoron* and the hybrid *R.lindleyi* x *R.sino-nuttallii* with very large white trumpet-shaped flowers. Notable here also are a large tree of *Weinmannia trichosperma* with large fern-like pinnate leaves, a large specimen of *Styrax hemsleyana* with spikes of white orange-blossom-like flowers in late May and June, also *Magnolia globosa*, flowering about the same time. Also in this garden are the tender *Clethra arborea* from Madeira, only successful otherwise in the South West of Ireland and in the Isles of Scilly. The flowers are like lilies of the valley. There is also an unusual purple-flowered form of *Erica canaliculata* flowering in March and early April.

The next garden (6 on map) has again more tender plants, particularly the rare *Acacia implexa* against the wall and also *Luculia gratissima* from the Himalaya which has large panicles of pale blush pink flowers and is very sweetly scented but which is usually only grown as a greenhouse plant in Britain. Another of the same kind is *Dodonaea viscosa* which has purplish-maroon foliage. Conspicuous in this garden is the purple-leaved form of *Cordyline australis* 'Atropurpurea' with narrow sword like leaves. The New Zealanders call it their 'Cabbage tree'. Against the wall is the passion flower *Passiflora coerulea* which fruits freely in the summer. Here there are masses of fuchsias to provide summer colour and also the unusual *Fuchsia excorticata* with peeling bark but in flower rather disappointing. It is a native of New Zealand. The sweet-scented *Pittosporum tobira* with its thick leathery leaves comes from China and Japan but is very commonly planted as hedges in

Mediterranean countries. It grows adequately though against a wall in other counties such as Sussex, but here grows larger.

In the last small walled garden there are two valuable summer-flowering shrubs with bright yellow flowers *Cassia corymbosa* from South America and *Fremontodendron californicum* from California. Both are most decorative and have a long-flowering season. There is a large specimen of *Magnolia* x *highdownensis* which has large pendulous white flowers like small umbrellas with masses of red stamens in the centre. This is a flower at which you should look from below if possible. It originally occurred in Cornwall at Caerhayes Castle. The other part of this area is used as kitchen garden and is not open to the public. As one leaves this wonderful series of walled gardens there is a conspicuous plant of the bright scarlet rhododendron 'Elizabeth', flowering in late April and May, one of the numerous good plants raised at Bodnant, also the pink form of *Raphiolepis umbellata* from Japan which has a long flowering season from April into June. There is also a good specimen of the rather tender *R.maddenii* which has large trumpet shaped white flowers flushed with pink in late May and early June. It is one of the finest species of its series.

Resisting temptations to stray across the drive to the delights of the stream garden one comes to a meadow area still on the right of the drive, known sometimes as Queen Elizabeth's meadow from the royal-planted trees. Queen Elizabeth the Queen Mother planted there in 1962 a lovely specimen of the Bhutan pine, *P.wallichiana* with its long drooping needles of bluish green, one of the most beautiful species. It is now a flourishing tree of 20 ft or more. The Princess Anne planted in 1972 the more tender *Pinus patula* from Mexico with long bright green drooping needles while older trees of royal association are a fine oak, planted to commemorate Queen Victoria's Diamond Jubilee in 1897 and a lime planted in 1901 to commemorate King Edward VII's Coronation. A great feature of this area is a large tree of *Paulownia tomentosa*, which used to be known as *P.imperialis*. It forms its buds in late autumn but does not open the clusters of lovely mauve foxglove-like flowers till the following late April or May, providing the winter has not been too severe. Later it develops massive leaves often a foot across like an elephant's ear. Some lovely Japanese maples are spaced about the meadow and at present the trees are still small enough to be seen well. Here is another tree of *Magnolia campbellii* and also the Yulan *M.denudata* and the early-flowering *M.stellata*. On the edge of the meadow are a large *Embothrium* and banks of the bright red *R.*'Shilsonii', a hybrid of *R.barbatum* x *R.thomsonii* and one of the best of the early-flowering hybrids, surpassing in brightness of colour the older 'Cornish Red', an old *arboreum* hybrid which is near it.

The drive between the meadow and the house has some very fine rhododendrons. Early to flower in March and early April are the large-leaved *R.grande* with big heads of white or pink-tinted flowers. A little further up the drive is a fine group of *R.mallotum*, the underside of whose leaves is bright rusty in colour. The flowers are deep crimson. Here also is the more tender *R.rhabdotum*, one of the *Maddenii* series with white trumpets streaked down the centre of the lobes of the corolla with five deep red stripes. It is unique in this character among the rhododendrons we can grow. Other large-leaved rhododendrons include a large tree well over 20 ft tall of the rare *R.sinogrande boreale* whose leaves, shiny above, sometimes measure 2 ft in length and 1 ft wide. The flowers are creamy-white and waxy and the heads nearly a foot across, borne in late March or early April, usually a little later than those of the yellower *R. macabeanum*. There are several specimens of these also on the drive but they have been cut back to encourage greater bushiness. One should not miss a group of a fine form of the deciduous *R.schlippen-bachii* with flowers like pink butterflies, also the brilliant scarlet *R.neriiflorum*, a good compact group owing to early pruning of which the late Sir Edward Bolitho was a great advocate. He applied it also very severely to large groups near the house of the later *R.griersonianum*, so that the effect was a most brilliant mass of colour rivalling a bed of scarlet geraniums, also to the group of a very fine scarlet form, raised in this garden, of *R.*'Fusilier', so well named. Here also are groups of both the blue and the white *Olearia* x *scilloniensis* like aristocratic michaelmas daisies in early summer.

In the courtyard around the porch of the house are groups of the very early-flowering *R.* x *praecox* whose magenta-pink flowers usually open in March, frost permitting and the later flowering *R.yunnanense* with white or purple-tinged flowers and the pale yellow *R.campylocarpum*. There are also masses of the evergreen azaleas 'Hinomayo' and 'Hinodegiri', all kept compact by severe pruning. The same treatment is applied successfully to the often rather lanky rhododendron 'Lady Alice Fitzwilliam' with its beautiful scented white trumpet-shaped flowers. There is a background of the bright green evergreen *Griselinia littoralis* from New Zealand and also from the same country *Olearia paniculata*, still perhaps better known as *O.forsteri*, and a good hedging plant in really mild areas. It is a winter flowering plant but the flowers are not conspicuous although well scented. On the porch of the house, which is not open to the public, is twined the tender *Lapageria rosea* from Chile whose large bright crimson bells are a great beauty in summer. To the courtyard and to the woods near the house there is a splendid background of tall mature beeches which keep off much of the wind and add greatly to the garden.

Going round the house to the left there are some very tender plants including the only specimen I know growing outside in mainland Britain of the rich purple-flowered *Tibouchina urvilliana*, from Brazil, much better known as *T.semidecandra*. The flowers are large and very brilliant in colour in late summer and early autumn. It is partly protected by a very large scarlet lobster claw plant *Clianthus puniceus* from New Zealand and close by is the yellow-flowered bottle brush *Callistemon pithioides*. Here also is the climbing yellow poppy *Dendromecon rigida*, the flowers so well complemented by the glaucous foliage. I also noted here the very tender *Datura sanguinea* which bears large hanging trumpets of orange-red in late summer. It is the only specimen of it that I know growing outside in mainland Britain. I say mainland so as to exclude the Isles of Scilly and the Channel Islands. One should not pass in a hurry also the yellow mimosa *Acacia verticillata* with its prickly needle-like leaves or the sweetly scented *Pittosporum tobira* or even more unusual a bed of the Chatham Island forget-me-not *Myosotidium hortensia*. This is one of the choicest plants in the garden and has large fleshy green leaves and in spring spikes of bright blue flowers, about 2 ft high. It grows in its native habitat in the Antipodes near the shore and is always presumed to thrive best when given a good annual mulch of sea weed or decayed fish.

Passing the house and a fine compact bank of the dwarf *Saluenense* and Lapponicum rhododendrons, a brilliant sight in late April and May with its many bright mauve species such as *R. impeditum* and *R.scintillans*, one comes to another magnolia garden surrounded by a low wall. Here is probably the finest magnolia in the garden, a very large tree, far overtopping the wall, of *M. sargentiana robusta* with thousands of purplish pink flowers in late

March and early April. In 1976 it measured about 40 ft high and 48 ft across and was branched from the base and may well be the largest in the country and the one by which an early spring visitor is likely to remember the garden. As a background and providing shelter from the the south west, the direction of the most frequent winds, is a vast plant of the large-leaved evergreen *Magnolia delavayi*, flowering much later but tending to hide its flowers among the leaves, and a group of *Eucryphia cordifolia* with unusually large leaves and about 50 ft tall, a fine sight in July and August. Around the big magnolia are some very choice and tender rhododendrons, a very large but still thick bush of *R.taggianum* about 7 ft tall by 6 ft across and flowering in early May, and another of *R.megacalyx* about the same size, both with white trumpets nearly 6 in. long. Near is a very fine bush of a choice pink *R.maddenii*, and flowering earlier in March and early April are the yellow and more dwarf *R.*'Golden Oriole Talavera' and the paler yellow *R.*'Velaspis'. Here also is the very tender *R.stenaulum* of the *Stamineum* series with funnel shaped pale lilac-pink flowers tinged violet inside, usually flowering in April. In summer as one leaves this magnolia garden look over the low wall to one's left to see a very large plant of *Hoheria lyallii* with masses of white flowers in July. The little garden in which it grows is close to the house and is one of the very few parts kept private.

From the lawn in front of the house one can get good views down to the bay and St Michael's Mount. On the lawn is a large three-trunked *Myrtus luma* (also known as *apiculata*) with lovely bright mahogany peeling bark, about 20 ft tall and flowering with pearl-like flowers in late summer. This produces abundant self-sown seedlings in many Cornish gardens. On the other side of the lawn are two tall magnolias *M.campbellii mollicomata* and *M.* 'Charles Raffill' a hybrid of *campbellii* and its var. *mollicomata*. Both are about 50 ft tall and usually flower freely late in March. Behind is a large tree, about 40 ft tall of *Schima khasiana* which is usually covered with white flowers in late summer. It is too tender though for colder gardens. Near here are groups of some very good forms of *Rhododendron albrechtii* and *R.schlippenbachii*, two very beautiful deciduous members of the *Azalea* series. As one enters the woodland garden one finds some very large hybrids and forms of *R. arboreum*, flowering early, some in March and a little later, an old and venerable giant *R.falconeri* planted about 1897, now about 35 ft tall and as much across, usually covered in late April with large heads of creamy flowers. Notice the rusty covering of the underneath of the large leaves. Near it is also an old *R.griffithianum*, one of the original Hooker rhododendrons from the Himalaya. It has lovely clear white flowers. It is usually recognisable by its drooping leaves. Other large-leaved species in this area include *R.sinogrande*, *R.calophytum* and *R.magnificum*. Too tender for most gardens is a tall slender tree of the very large-leaved *Magnolia rostrata*, whose big white flowers come out with the leaves about July. It is now about 30 ft high.

Another notable plant here is a very good pink form of *R. lanigerum*, which has received an RHS Award of Merit and usually flowers in late March or April. It is close to *R.arboreum* but the undersides of the leaves are covered with more indumentum. At the upper end of the wood are many camellias among which 'Salutation' a pale salmon-pink *reticulata* hybrid is very fine in March. Before coming out to the drive one should not miss in late March and early April the magnificent FCC plant of *Rhododendron macabeanum*, which is now 20 ft or more tall and as wide and has very large trusses of yellow flowers. It is one of the finest plants in the garden.

Descending the drive on one's right hand side is the stream garden, whose banks are thick with candelabra primulas of all sorts, purple *japonica*, yellow *helodoxa* and *prolifera* and *florindae* followed in June with blue meconopsis while all the ground is covered with bluebells in May. In early summer this is a beautiful part of the garden, while later it is bright blue with masses of hydrangeas. The white arum lilies and earlier the yellow *Lysichitum*, the skunk cabbages, abound. The golden shrubby hypericum 'Rowallane' flowers from June to November and sometimes even through the winter too and is undoubtedly the finest of its genus but too tender for cold gardens. The numerous tree ferns give this part of the garden a lush and exotic appearance. Here they flourish. Here also are great bushes of the lovely white *Rhododendron johnstoneanum*, its double form and its supposed pink hybrid with *R.tephropeplum*, the odd double 'Johnnie Johnston' which also received the RHS Award of Merit. Planted back from the drive is that unusual but very decorative form of the Lawson cypress known as 'Intertexta' now about 30 ft tall with drooping green fern-like branchlets (2 on map).

As one emerges again at the entrance one realises what an exceptionally rich garden this is and with what adventurous skill it was planted by that great Cornish character the late Colonel Sir Edward Bolitho, who served the county as Lord Lieutenant and Chairman of the County Council for many years, also how well it is now maintained by his son Major Simon Bolitho, the National Trust and their young but very skilled head gardener Mr Peter Horder, formerly a Wisley student. I am much indebted to them for their help. I have only mentioned a proportion of the interesting plants. There are many more.

Tresco Abbey Gardens,
Isles of Scilly

Mr R.A. Dorrien Smith

Isles of Scilly by helicopter or boat from Penzance, then by boat from St Mary's (20 minutes) to Carn Near landing, then 15 minutes walk. Gardens open daily except Sundays when entry is restricted to Islanders. House to be opened in 1977. A unique garden made by four generations of Smiths and Dorrien Smiths with large collection of tender plants many collected by owner's family. Soil acid over granite shale and shillet. Rainfall about 32 in.

It was in 1834 that Augustus Smith, a Hertfordshire squire, took over the lease of the Isles of Scilly from the Duchy of Cornwall and started to build his house on Tresco by the site of an ancient Abbey. He must have been a very remarkable man, interested in political ideas and education and anxious to try out his theories. He became literally in deed and name Lord Proprietor of the Isles. He built schools and charged a penny to go to school and two pennies to stay away, a very effective scheme. He also started the gardens which have become famous throughout the world and planted the first shelter belts on which the gardens depend. He planted *Pinus radiata* and *Cupressus macrocarpa*, from California, both very wind-resistant and hedges, now 30 ft tall, of *Quercus ilex*. He also built great walls of granite. On the lee side of a small hill he planted sycamores, elms, oaks and poplars. His garden was made on the southern and windward side of the hill and was planned on a grid system, long terraces, following the contours of the hill and connecting steep paths and steps. When he came there was little other than gorse and heather and no trees. Out of twelve acres he carved his magnificent garden which grew in his lifetime into a most unusual collection and his successors extended it into the woodland behind. He collected plants from far and wide, particularly from the southern hemisphere and found that they flourished exceedingly. The climate is unusually favourable. It is almost frost free although up to 7°F have been recorded but rarely. My first visit to the garden followed one of these frosts and my host, Major A.A. Dorrien Smith was sad, but the effect did not last. There is ample rainfall, although on the average 10 in. less annually than at Penzance. An unusual feature, however, is the very high humidity, about 90 per cent on the average. This with the sun and the sea air and the well drained top soil has made everything grow very fast. One visitor described it as like the big greenhouse at Kew with the roof off. Another comparison might be with the richer Riviera gardens, but there is greater variety of plants at Tresco especially those from New Zealand, Australia, South Africa and South America. Even the knowledgeable gardener will feel it a strange world in which he knows few of the plants, but their magnificence, luxuriance and beauty will surely impress him and tempt him to come again and learn more. There is nowhere else in the British Isles in any way like it. We owe a great debt to the Dorrien Smith family not only for its planting but also for its preservation. Augustus Smith lived till 1872 and was succeeded by his nephew Lieut Algernon Dorrien Smith, another great gardener, who enlarged the garden and started the growing of the polyanthus Narcissus in particular the sweet-scented 'Scilly White' and 'Soleil d'Or', for their early flowering and this proved the most remunerative of the Islands' industries, only to be superseded in recent years by tourism. Others were grown too but these two were the most successful. He found them originally growing among the ruins of the old Abbey. Mr Algernon Dorrien Smith died in 1918 and was succeeded by his son Major Arthur Dorrien Smith who had already made several plant collecting expeditions to the islands round New

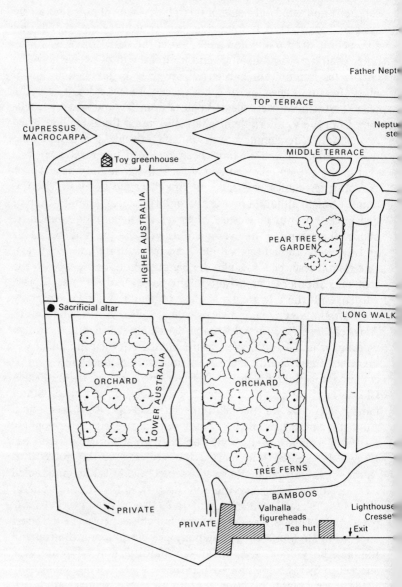

Father Nept

TOP TERRACE

CUPRESSUS
MACROCARPA

Neptu
ste

MIDDLE TERRACE

Toy greenhouse

PEAR TREE
GARDEN

HIGHER AUSTRALIA

Sacrificial altar

LONG WALK

ORCHARD

ORCHARD

LOWER AUSTRALIA

TREE FERNS

BAMBOOS

PRIVATE

Valhalla
figureheads

Lighthouse
Cresse

PRIVATE

Tea hut

Exit

TRESCO ABBEY GARDENS

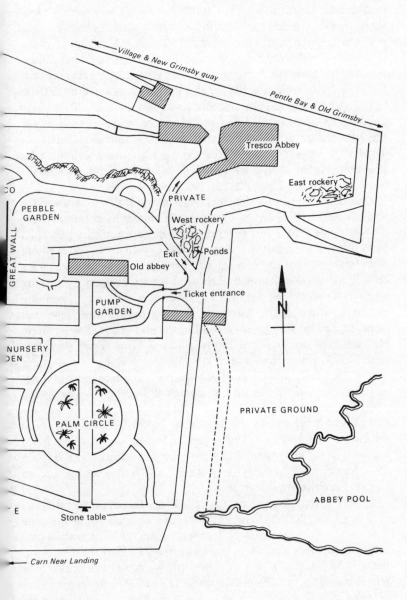

Village & New Grimsby quay

Pentle Bay & Old Grimsby

Tresco Abbey

East rockery

PEBBLE GARDEN

GREAT WALL

PRIVATE

West rockery

Exit — Ponds

Old abbey

N

PUMP GARDEN

Ticket entrance

NURSERY EN

PRIVATE GROUND

PALM CIRCLE

ABBEY POOL

Stone table

Carn Near Landing

Zealand and Australia including the Chatham Islands and sent back seeds and plants for the gardens at Tresco including *Olearia semi-dentata*, which still thrives in the garden. He wrote accounts of these expeditions for the Kew Bulletin and plates of many of the plants were published in the Botanical Magazine. Many plants came to Tresco direct from Kew and also from his great friend Canon Boscawen of Ludgvan Rectory, one of the great gardeners of the day. Major Dorrien Smith died in 1955 and was succeeded by his son Lt Cdr T.A. Dorrien Smith, another most enthusiastic and ebullient gardener who continued the tradition and travelled and added much to the garden. Unfortunately he died rather prematurely in 1974 and was succeeded by his son Mr R.A. Dorrien Smith who now controls the garden with the help of a young and enthusiastic head gardener Mr Peter Clough. No state aid is received.

One enters by a gate near the bottom and quickly passes a dell with *Crinum bulbispermum* (*C.capense*) in masses in autumn. These are very pale pink and the flowers are more rounded when open than those of the hybrid *C*. x *powellii* and I prefer them. Everywhere there are agapanthus naturalised, even in the windswept grass outside the garden. Another plant that is very frequent is the blue *Convolvulus mauretanicaus*, making mats over the rocks. Then one climbs up through the garden to the top terrace and Neptune's steps, topped by a large stone head of the god. Just below Neptune one passes on the right the largest plant of *Metrosideros tomentosa* from New Zealand, now a large tree of 80 ft or more and as much across. Curiously aerial roots hang from the top like those of a fig. In June it is covered with deep crimson flowers and is one of the great sights of the garden. It is reported that it can be seen from far out at sea. It belongs to the *Myrtaceae* and unfortunately it is too tender for most gardens. The large rounded masses of spine tipped leaves, 4 or 5 ft across, beside the path are dasylirions, *D.acrotrichum* from Mexico, and have spikes of white bell-like flowers and are an unusual architectural feature.

From the top of the steps one can turn either right towards the rock wall and the house or left along the top walk. Near here the rare and tender *Eucalyptus ficifolia* with scarlet flowers was blooming in September and there are more trees of it in the woodland behind. As far as I know this is the only garden in the British Isles where it flowers satisfactorily outside. Here too are the giant spikes of *Agave salmiana*. This species comes from Mexico and some were

60–80 years old and the candelabra like spikes 30 ft tall. There is also the more common *Agave americana* which one sees so frequently in Riviera gardens. Towards the house there are the big spikes of the *Furcraea longaeva* from Mexico. These have tall spikes with pendulous flowers of greenish white looking like a green cascade surrounding the stem and are most conspicuous. The rosette is like that of a large yucca. In 1976 there were 60 spikes in flower. Behind them the hill rises in a rocky wall which has been planted with succulent plants some of which have naturalised themselves. There is the small spinous *Aloe arborescens* with scarlet flowers, masses of *Aeonium cuneatum* from the Canary Islands and also many other species, some with rosettes with dark maroon brown leaves at the end of long snaking stems. They look like the rosettes of large sempervivums, the houseleeks, or sometimes they are flattened like a large saucer. The flowers are yellow or pinkish and are borne in large spikes, but in other areas they need cool greenhouse treatment. Along the terrace, which is very colourful for most of the summer, there are numerous pelargoniums in flower and among them project the great spikes of *Beschorneria yuccoides* creeping like gigantic pink animals over the pelargoniums. Beside the path are many other rare plants, tree heaths such as *Erica diaphana* with its pale pink flowers from South Africa, hybrid watsonias from South Africa, brilliant in colour in the autumn like more delicate gladioli and some old hybrid *Amaryllis belladonna* like 'Kewensis' lovely pink trumpets in great clusters. Here also flower some of the proteas from South Africa, the giant *P.cynaroides* with flowers up to 8 in. across, the lovely pink *P.barbigera* and *P.compacta* which grows here best of all the proteas. It has been found that the proteas associate well with tree heaths.

The pin cushion leucospermums also grow here with many other South African plants. The silver tree *Leucodendron argenteum* has not flowered although it is 30 ft tall but is attractive with its silvery leaves and there are also the rarely seen *L.decorum* and *L.discolor*. St Catherine's lace *Eriogonum giganteum* with its grey foliage comes from California but has settled down well here. On this terrace are also the rare *Banksias* from Australia with their curious flowerheads like little prickly erect barrels on the branches.

As one descends again to the middle terrace one passes two fine specimens of a date palm from the Canary Islands, *Phoenix canariensis*, with graceful arching leaves sometimes 15 to 20 ft long. On the middle terrace is a great show throughout the year, especially in the early summer when the giant echiums and the golden cytisus are in flower. The echiums are relations of our wild viper's bugloss but the spikes grow to 20 ft in some cases, in others they branch into many stems in varying shades of blue and mauve, since many hybrids have developed over the years and the bluest have been selected. There is also the pink *Echium wildprettii*. The hybrids have been named *E.scilloniensis* and the best blue 'Tresco Blue', derived largely from *E.fastuosum*. It is worth pausing to look at a fine specimen of the scarlet flowered *Grewia sutherlandii* from Natal. The flowers are clustered in large heads each with a black disc and I know of no better specimen even in a Riviera garden. The terrace and also Neptune's steps are bright with many scarlet aloes which begin flowering about Christmas and later come masses of mesembryanthemums, used as a composite name for several genera and many species, but making cascades of deep pink, magenta and even orange over the rocks. There are also *Venidiums*, *Arctotis*, *Venidio-Arctotis* and *Gazanias* in great abundance. The dimorphothecas are very fine and a particular dark purple one known as 'Tresco Peggy' has occurred and been selected here. On this terrace also is the fearsome group of *Puya chilensis*. Some flower spikes of 9 ft are produced every year but 1966 was a bumper year with 23 spikes and the group is now 30 ft × 15 ft and the leaves stiff and spiny and used by the American Indians for fish hooks. The flowers are greenish yellow sticking out among silvery perches for the pollinating humming birds. There are also other species with blue flowers in the garden such as *P.alpestris*, more dwarf, and *P.berteroniana*.

One can descend the Neptune steps again to the Long Walk which forms the lowest terrace; on the left is an arch of the old Abbey with a rock garden around and curiously bananas *Musa basjoo* with enormous pale green leaves, while on the right the wall has many treasures. There are the large rosettes of *Doreanthes palmeri* a very imposing feature in the border. The leaves are 4 ft long and the great spikes after 12 ft in height, scarlet with funnel-shaped flowers. It is a native of Queensland in Australia. Further along is a splendid grove of *Myrtus luma*, still known as *M.apiculata*, whose bark is a clear ochreous yellow when the outer layer has peeled off. It makes a distinctive feature and here the trunks have been left close together and so have grown up without side branches. Coming from Chile it is tender in cold areas but in the South West grows well. It flowers in late summer usually a little later than the common myrtle. Near is another fine *Metrosideros tomentosa*. The garden also contains fine specimens of *M.robusta*, the 'rata' of New Zealand which also has bright crimson flowers.

As early as January and often at Christmas the garden is gay with yellow mimosa, *Acacia baileyana*, and other species. Later the *Cordylines* flower. There are many trees of the narrow leaved *C. australis* which have great clusters of whitish flower and some of *C.indivisa* with wider leaves, one of the most beautiful foliaged plants I know. *Geranium maderense* and *G.palmatum* from Madeira make great heads of purplish pink flowers all through the summer 4 ft tall and also fine rosettes. Against the wall look out for the orange and red flower heads in large clusters of the climbing amaryllid from Ecuador called bomarea. It is a most striking plant. Near the foot of the Neptune steps also are more palms such as *Rapalostylis sapoa*. Near the myrtle grove is a group of the tall *Lobelia gibberoa* from the equatorial mountains of East Africa whose spikes I have seen measuring 29 ft, grey green with blue flowers emerging between the bracts.

If the visitor has time he should also walk along the drive to the Abbey and through the wood on each side of it. Here are tree ferns, mostly *Dicksonia antarctica* but also the more tender cyatheas. There are more eucalyptus including the scarlet-flowered *E.ficifolia* and the tender *Clethra arborea* from Madeira which has spikes of white bell-like flowers like lilies of the valley. One should also visit the Valhalla Museum where the figureheads of old ships wrecked on the islands have been collected, repaired and repainted to their original gaudiness.

I have only discussed a small proportion of the many unusual plants here. Tresco is like a great botanical garden with plants from so many areas that it is unique, a most valuable storehouse of plants especially of those from the southern hemisphere and many growing as well as in the native land. The plants are well labelled and one should come again or stay at the Island Hotel or the New Inn since one visit is not enough.

Trewithen

Mr Michael Galsworthy

Between Grampound and Probus on A390, 1½ miles E of Probus, 6 miles
NE of Truro, white gate on right coming from Truro, signposted. Open
Monday to Saturday (including Bank Holidays) 2.30–4.30 pm from
beginning March–end October, except during July and August. House,
early Georgian dating from 1723, open Thursday only. Teas available,
also garden shop with many choice plants at reasonable prices. Garden
made by the late Mr G.H. Johnstone, OBE, VMH, now owned by grand-
son of Mr Johnstone, particularly distinguished for its design and large
collection of magnolias, camellias and rhododendrons. On heavy loam
enriched with layers of leaf mould, about 25 acres. Rainfall average.

Without doubt Trewithen is one of the finest gardens in this county
of fine gardens, both for its bold design, for the large collection of
very choice mature plants and for the excellent state of their
cultivation. Mr George Johnstone was particularly keen on the
Asiatic magnolias and planted every kind that was available. He was
the author of that magnificent book *Asiatic Magnolias in Cultivation*
published in 1955 by the Royal Horticultural Society but now
unfortunately out of print. Early in his life he suffered a severe
hunting accident and thereafter was confined to a wheeled chair
in the garden but he had great courage and persistence and always
got to the parts he wanted and directed the operations. He also had
an unusually fine eye for placing his plants to their best effect.

The main feature of the garden is a long lawn with undulating
edges stretching away from the house for over 200 yards and 36
yards wide at the house end. It was made after the first war when
the trees were cut. One enters from the courtyard at the side of the
house through a walled garden with some choice plants on the
walls. The *Clianthus puniceus* is enormous, right up to the top of the
wall. At the end a wisteria goes up into an old yew. Then one goes
through a small door into the main woodland garden. Immediately
in front is a fine bank 10 ft or more high of *Pieris formosa forrestii*,
scarlet in its young leaves with cascades of white lily of the valley

type flowers. Among it are banks of rhododendron 'Trewithen Orange', one of the finest hybrids raised at Trewithen, from *concatenans* x 'Full House'. It has orange bell-shaped flowers. *R.*'Chrysomanicum' is also here, one of the finest of the yellow flowered tender hybrids, a cross between *R.chrysodoron* and *R.burmanicum*. Against the wall are such tender species of *R.rhabdotum*, with lily-like flowers each with a red streak down the centre of the petal. Then one passes a large *Davidia involucrata* and comes out at the corner of the lawn with on the right a 30 ft mass of *Griselinia littoralis*. One realises then the size of the beeches which dominate and shelter the garden and on which it so largely depends. It is best to go down the right hand side of the lawn and back by the other. First there is a large *M.liliflora*, but dominating it all is a 50 ft *M.campbellii* subsp. *mollicomata* hanging over the lawn. This is a good pink form and is beautiful in early spring, one of the finest trees that I know of this subspecies. Slightly earlier and so more vulnerable to frost is a tree of *M.campbellii*, a good deep pink form just behind and to the side of the *mollicomata*. A recent measurement gave it 64 ft. There is also a pale form of this species in the garden, the one illustrated in Mr Johnstone's book.

Returning to the lawn one comes to a large *M.* x *soulangiana* and beyond *Corylopsis platypetala*. This used to be a vast plant layered down all round but it was severely cut back a few years ago. It will soon have filled the space it formerly occupied. Mr Johnstone used to regard this as the finest of the *Corylopsis* and it was certainly magnificent with long yellow tassels of flower in early spring, about the same time as the *Magnolia mollicomata*. Beyond it a new bay has been made where a tree has been taken out and filled with young plants of rhododendrons. Everywhere one feels that the garden is still alive, young plants are mixed with old, and the best of the newer rhododendrons are still coming into the garden. *R.*'Alison Johnstone', (*concatenans* x *yunnanense*) one of the finest hybrids raised by Mr Johnstone and named after his wife is here, a mass of translucent pearly pink flowers, also some more plants of 'Trewithen Orange' and a seedling from it raised by Captain Collingwood Ingram and named 'George Johnstone'. Towards the end of the lawn there are some fine nothofagus, the South American beech, and a deodar cedar. *Magnolia cylindrica* is also here and has made an 8 ft tree, flowering freely.

Coming back up the other side one should not fail to note

Viburnum betulifolium, with hanging clusters of fruit in the autumn. This is one of the finest groups I know of this. Then there are stems of two excellent birches, *B.utilis* and *B.utilis* x *maximowiczii*, this latter a deep maghogany; both have a large girth and stand out from a distance across the lawn, showing the value of such bark. Further up is a large group of *Magnolia stellata* and another of the special plants of the garden *Rehderodendron macrocarpum*. It is over 36 ft tall now and has white bells like those of a *Halesia* or a *Styrax* to which it is closely related. The fruits though are large and woody. It was only introduced from China in 1934 and a mature tree only exists in two gardens, Trewithen and Maidwell Hall in Northamptonshire. It is, however, now being distributed from Trewithen. Almost opposite it a small path leads out of the side of the lawn bringing one to a path bordered by hydrangeas, lovely and colourful in the autumn. Here also are the gigantic plants of *Rhododendron macabeanum*, another of the beauties of the garden. It is an exceptionally fine form, a deep yellow with a compact truss. The largest tree is 25 ft high and has a spread of 35 ft while beside it is a propagated plant nearly as large. This was grown from seed collected in Manipur by Kingdon Ward and it is undoubtedly one of the finest of the large-leaved species. Beyond it is a selected group of *Camellia japonica* and *williamsii* varieties. I particularly liked 'Glen's Orbit', a pink semi-double rather like 'Donation'. It was named on the day when Cdr Glen made his first orbit round the moon and is placed near 'Donation' for comparison. Another very fine one was *C.japonica* 'Auburn White', a perfectly formed double. It sheltered behind 'Drama Girl', a large red semi-double. 'Donation' itself has grown into a tall bush 20 ft tall and so floriferous that it is weighed down. Behind it is a vast group of *Eucryphia cordifolia* which must be now over 50 ft tall. The four or five plants have grown together to make a great evergreen mass which in late July and August is covered with white flowers.

Here a dell with tree ferns leads down and on the other side is a fine tree of *Magnolia sprengeri diva,* a beautiful pink in mid-March. Other good magnolias in the garden include several of *mollicomata*, including the very dark 'Lanarth', several *M.sargentiana robusta* of rather varying shades of purplish-pink and *M.dawsoniana*. Beside the dell is a bank of forms of *Camellia saluenensis*, which flower over a long period and are very variable. Selected forms of it have been propagated and planted about the garden. The wild single forms of

C.reticulata also grow well at Trewithen and several have been named. One of the finest is 'Elizabeth Johnstone', a pale pink. Beyond the dell a new small garden has been made with choice plants such as rhododendron 'Michael's Pride', a creamy yellow trumpet derived from a cross between *R.dalhousiae* and *R.burmanicum* and one of the finest *Maddeniis, Pittosporum tenuifolium* 'Purpureum' and *P. eugenioides*.

Coming back towards the house one passes *Michelia doltsopa*, flowering well and large, such rhododendrons as 'Jack Skelton', **one of the finest hybrids raised at Trewithen**, *Schima khasiana*, a late flowering evergreen tree with flowers like those of a small camellia, and *Rhododendron lindleyi* growing in a ditch and well sheltered but of great beauty when in flower. *Enkianthus chinensis* was lovely with its greenish yellow and red bells like a ballet dancer while *Vaccinium retusum* was good with pink flowers in autumn. Coming back to the lawn again there was *Nothofagus procera* at the end, a fine specimen usually giving some good autumn tints. A young *Cupressus cashmeriana* had just been put out and was carefully wrapped for its first winter but it is quick growing and should form there a beautifully silvery-blue tree. Huge embothriums 30 ft tall are striking and floriferous, while quieter but lovely both in spring and autumn is *Euptelea pleisperma* (*E.franchetii*) and *Stewartia sinensis* which is here making a small tree with fine bark, flowering in mid summer. Unusual is *Acer laevigatum*, a fine maple but one rarely seen. But so rich is the garden that one can go on with naming choice and rare plants almost indefinitely.

It is indeed a magnificent garden and beautifully kept by Mr Michael Taylor and his staff, a fine tribute to Mr George Johnstone, a great plantsman, and Mrs Johnstone who keeps it so well and also keeps it ever young, always planting new and exciting plants **rather than resting on her laurels. Unfortunately she died in 1978.**

Some other Gardens Open to the Public

Blackpool House, Stoke Fleming, Nr Dartmouth, Devon. (Lady A. Newman.) $4\frac{1}{2}$ miles SW of Dartmouth. Open in aid of National Gardens Scheme by appointment any day, 2–6 pm. House not open. A garden of many unusual and tender trees and shrubs terraced on the steep hillside above Slapton Sands, a very exposed site open to salt spray. The garden is rather overgrown but look out for the tall blue spikes of the echiums in summer, some up to 10 ft, the row of old cork oak trees (*Quercus suber*) and some unusual succulents outdoors such as aloes and *Agave americana*. The blue forget-me-not from the Chatham Islands sometimes flowers here and there are enormous specimens of *Magnolia campbellii mollicomata* and eucryphias such as *E.cordifolia* and *E.billardieri*. The broad leaved *Cordyline indivisa* grows well here and at the top of the slope is a small water garden with tree ferns around and a *Magnolia campbellii* as well as a good view over the sea. The rainfall is very high.

Staplers, Sticklepath, Nr Okehampton, Devon. (Mrs Mary Lees.) On A30 about 3 miles E of Okehampton. No longer open to the public.

Combe Head, Bampton, Devon. (Mr and Mrs A. D. Baxter.) Off Bampton to Dulverton road. B.3222. Open daily throughout year by appointment in aid of National Gardens Scheme. A young arboretum planted on a fine sloping natural setting by present owners and maintained by their own efforts, 700 feet up. Combe Head contains a large collection which the owner estimates at over 2000 different trees and shrubs, arranged by genera and largely grown in blocks. Tender acacias such as *A.pravissima* and *A. verticillata* and a fine mimosa *A.dealbata* are notable and also trees with fine bark such as *Acer griseum, Betula utilis, Prunus serrula* and *Arbutus menziesii* are promising and will make a striking feature when they mature. There is also an interesting collection of old shrub roses at their best in June. Each specimen is planted with a generous amount of manure or compost and then the growth around is kept down with herbicides such as Grammoxone, which doesn't look very attractive but is a practical method of looking after a large collection.

Tapeley Park, Instow, Devon. (The Christie Estate Trust.) 5 miles SW of Barnstaple. On A39 between Barnstaple and Bideford. May–mid-September. Daily except Mondays and Saturdays, but open Bank Holidays 2–6 pm. House not open. An Italian-style garden in a warm protected area, though now much simplified. On one side of the fine Georgian-style house, steps lead down through yews clipped to form a solid covering. The first terrace gives a sub-tropical effect with cordylines while the lower one is planted with hardy palms (*Trachycarpus fortunei*) in rows along centre and sides. The bays between the buttresses of the terrace are planted with different colour schemes of roses while such tender shrubs on the walls as *Feijoa sellowiana* and deep yellow *Sophora tetraptera*, the kowhai tree from New Zealand provide added interest. At the end is a group of old *Pinus radiata* and other features included the statuary and carved pillars. Other notable plants included pots of white *Lilium speciosum* and an unusually large *Fabiana imbricata*.

Trerice, Nr Newlyn East, Cornwall. (The National Trust.) 3 miles SE of Newquay by A392 and A3058. Turn right at Kestle Mill. Open 1 April–31 October. Daily 2–6 pm. House also open. Garden has been newly planted but a fine walled courtyard in front of the house is striking with topiary on the lawn; planted under the walls are blue and purple and crimson hebes, *Escallonia monte-vidensis* with large white panicles of flower in late summer and early autumn, as well as other decorative foliage plants begins to look mature. A small orchard is growing up beside the house with apples, medlars and other fruits. The white *Rosa bracteata* was flowering late in summer against the house and other features are growing up to form a notable addition to a fine house.

Woodside, Higher Raleigh Road, Barnstaple, Devon. (Mr and Mrs Mervyn Feesey.) On outskirts of Barnstaple. A39 to Lynton cross-roads and about 300 yards from Fire Station. Open various Sundays in April–August in aid of National Gardens Scheme 2–7 pm, or at other times by appointment. House not open. A small garden, about $1\frac{1}{2}$ acres, on a sloping site and packed with unusual plants. Owner has particular interest in grasses and reeds, also plants from southern hemisphere. Many sempervivums and dwarf conifers, but many other plants as well. There were (September 1976 according to owner) 125 hebes, mostly dwarf, 25 potentillas, 35 sedums, approximately 400 ornamental grasses and 200 sedges. A collectors' garden of particular interest to those interested in plants of southern hemisphere and in grasses and dwarf conifers.

Index

Figure numbers refer to black and white illustrations. Plate numbers refer to colour illustrations.

Abelia floribunda, 97
Abies alba, 43, 74, 113
    cephalonica, 28, 43
    cephalonica 'Appolinis', 43
    cilicica, 43
    concolor, 43
    delavayi, 43
        var. *fabri*, 42
    grandis, 43
    homolepis, 43, 113
    magnifica, 43
    numidica, 43
    procera, 113
        'Glauca', 43
Abutilon 'Ashford Red', 45
    'Canary Bird', 117, 127
    megapotamicum, 92
    'Orange Glow', 118
    X *Suntense*, 118
    vitifolium, 118, 123
    vitifolium 'Tennant's White', 49
    vitifolium 'Veronica Tennant', 49
Acacia armata, 45
    baileyana, 141
    dealbata, 31, 58, 70, 79, 100, 101
    implexa, 128
    longifolia, 101
    melanoxylon, 81, 128
    pravissima, 66
    verticillata, 66, 79, 131
Acanthus, 97
Acer capillipes, 30
    distylum, 80
    griseum, 30, 32, 63, 77, 107, 123
    hookeri, 64
    japonicum, 37
        'Aureum', 77
    laevigatum, 145
    negundo 'Auratum', 43
    palmatum 'Osakazuki', 119
        'Senkaki', 63, 67, 73, 103
    pensylvanicum erythrocladum, 52
    pseudoplatanus 'Brilliantissimum', 119

Acidanthera, 66
Acland, Sir Richard, Sir Thomas, 53
Actinidia kolomikta, 47
Aeonium cuneatum, 139
Aesculus wilsoni, 90
Agapanthus, 76, 101, 110, 116, 138
Agave americana, 99, 139, 146, Fig. 22
    salmiana, 138
Akebia quinata, 45
Albizzia lophantha, 101
Alchemilla, 103
Alnus incana, 69
    rugosa, 44
    serrulata, 44
Aloe, 140, 146
    arborescens, 139
Aloysia citriodora, 102
Amaryllis belladonna, 45, 116, 139
    belladonna 'Kewensis', 139
Amory, Lady and Sir John, 17, 58, 65
Anthemis cupaniana, 77, 80
Antony House, garden at, 13, 16, 17, 85, Figs. 17, 18
Aralia, 47
    elata, 63, 77
Araliaceae, 43
Araucaria araucana, 113
Arbutus andrachne, 27
Arctostaphylos, 66
Arctotis, 140
Arlington Court, garden at, 21
Arnold Foster, 14
Artemisia, 103
    arborescens, 104
Arum, 75, 117, 133
Athrotaxis, 44
    cupressoides, 28
    selaginoides, 57, 105
Azara, 92
    dentata, 126
    microphylla, 58
    microphylla 'Variegata', 118

Baker, Mr. & Mrs. Ambrose, 17
Balfour, Professor Sir Isaac Bayley, 105
Ballota, 75
Bamboo, 98
Banksia, 15, 139
Bean, W.J., 79
Bedford, Dukes of, 39, 40, 42
Benmore, garden, 105
Berberidopsis corallina, 93
Berberis, 30, 39, 92
Bergenia, 58, 72
Beschorneria yuccoides, 104, 139
Betula *albo-sinensis*, 95, 107
    albo-sinensis var. *septentrionalis*, 44
    ermanii, 72, 95
    jacquemontii, 95
    utilis, 44, 144
    utilis X maximowiczii, 144
Bicton, garden at, 23, 79, Figs. 1, 2
Blackpool House, garden at, 146
Blake, Mr. P., 99
Bodnant, garden at, 122, 129
Bolitho, Lt. Col. Sir Edward, VMH, 123, 130, 134
Bolitho, Major Simon, 17, 123, 133
Bomarea, 141
Boscawen, Canon, 138
Bougainvillea, 26
Boyd, Viscount & Viscountess, 17, 102
Bressingham, gardens, 82
Brodick, garden, 105
Buckland Monachorum, The Garden House, garden at, 48, Figs. 8, 9, Pl. 2
Buddleia fallowiana, 103

Caerhays, garden at, 13, 15, 54, 88, 129, Pl. 4
Calceolaria integrifolia, 117
Callistemon, 68
    pithioides, 131
    speciosus, 26
Calocedrus decurrens, 111
Caltha polypetala, 66
Camellia 'Anticipation', 122
    'Beatrice Michael', 90
    'Brigadoon', 121
    'Caerhays', 90
    'Charles Michael', 90
    'Cornish Snow', 90, 97
    cuspidata, 76
    'Debbie', 121
    'Donation', 48, 54, 63, 117, 121, 122, 144, Fig. 25
    'Drama Girl', 144
    'Elizabeth Johnstone', 145
    'Else Jury', 122
    'Francis L', 122
    'George Blandford', 90

'Glen's Orbit', 144
'Henry Turnbull', 121
japonica, 30, 38, 76, 86, 87, 109, 121, 144
    'Adolphe Audusson', 144
    'Alba Plena', 52, 114, 118
    'Auburn White'. 144
    'Mercury', 73
    'Sylva', 51
'J.C. Williams', 90, 97, 98
'Margaret Waterhouse', 121
'Mary Christian', 90
'Preston Rose', 100
reticulata, 38, 66, 87, 109, 121, 122, 133, 145
    'Captain Rawes', 68, 90, 92, 100, 109
'Rosemary Williams', 90
'St. Ewe', 90
saluenensis, 86, 87, 144
'Salutation', 54, 133
sasanqua, 86, 97
    'Narumi-gata', 38
'Ville de Nantes', 100
williamsii, 38, 54, 73, 86, 87, 90, 94, 109, 117, 121, 144
Campbell-Watson, Mrs., 69
Campsis, 117
    chinensis, 47
Cane, Percy, 37, 39
Carclew, garden at, 91, Figs. 19–21
Carew Pole, Sir John and the late Lady, 17, 86
Carnation, 98
Carpobrotus, 14, 116
Carya ovata, 87, Fig. 18
Caryopteris, 102
Cassia corymbosa, 68, 70, 116, 129
Castle Drogo, garden at, 29
Castle Hill, garden at, 31, Fig. 4
Catalpa bignonioides, 27
Ceanothus, 36, 64, 68, 97
    impressus, 39
        'Puget Blue', 71
    'Indigo', 119
    'Trewithen Blue', 82, 98, 118, 120
Cedar of Lebanon, 45, 111
Cedrus atlantica, 111
    'Glauca', 41
    deodar, 26, 143
Celmisia, 63
Cephalotaxus, 28, 44
Ceratostigma willmottianum, 119
Cercidiphyllum japonicum, 38, 77
Cercis siliquastrum, 97, 104, 117
Chamaecyparis lawsoniana
    'Filiformis', 28
    lawsoniana 'Pendula', 41
        'Wisselii', 28, 46

Chamaecyparis (cont.)
  obtusa, 111
  pisifera 'Filifera', 57
Chichester, Miss Rosalie, 21
Chionodoxa, 63
Chope, Judge and Mrs., 17, 91
Chyverton, garden at, 93
Cineraria, 117
Cinnamomum camphora, 79
Cistus, 74, 103
Claytonia siberica, 21
Clematis, 68
  armandii, 70, 78
  'Etoile Violette', 66
  'Gravetye Beauty', 66
  heracleifolia 'Wyevale', 49
  indivisa, 51, 127, Fig. 8
  montana, 37
  texensis 'Duchess of Albany', 66
  trichotomum, 101
Clethra alnifolia, 39
  arborea, 128, 141
Clianthus puniceus, 66, 79, 101, 131, 142
Clifden, Lord, 108
Clinton, Lord, 23
Clough, Mr. Peter, 138
Codrington, Mr. John, 74
Colletia cruciata, 80
Collingwood-Ingram, Captain, 71, 72, 95, 143
Colutea arborescens, 49
Combe Head, 146
Comber, H., 13
Conifers, 23
Convolvulus cneorum, 102
  mauretanicus, 117, 138
Copeland, Mr. Ronald & Mrs., 118
Cordyline, 98, 141, 146
  australis, 16, 141
    'Atropurpurea', 128
  indivisa, 16, 141, 146
Cornus, 68
  capitata, 37, 72, 77, 79, 82, 97, 100
  florida, 39
    'Rubra', 82, 87
  kousa, 39, 72, 109
  nuttallii, 39, 54, 72, 109
Corokia macrocarpa, 118
Correa harisii, 117
Corylopsis platypetala, 70, 143
  spicata, 39
  willmottiae, 39
Cosmos atrosanguineus, 49
Cotehele, garden at, 96, Fig. 3
Cotinus Coggygria, 30, 96
Cotoneaster frigidus, 111
  lacteus, 49
County, Demonstration Garden and Arboretum, 98

Cox, Mr. Peter, 73
Crataegus X carrieri, 82
Crinodendron, 16
  hookeranum, 47, 75, 78
Crinum bulbispermum, 79, 138
  capense, 79
  X powellii, 45, 118, 138
Crocosmea 'Solfatare', 32, 104
Crocus, 146
  tomasinianus, 37
Cryptomeria, 105
  japonica, 27, 28, 100, 113, 118
    'Cristata', 112
    'Gracilis', 41
    'Spiralis', 46
Cunninghamia, 44
  lanceolata, 105, 112
  sinensis, 100
Cupressocyparis leylandii, 48, 73
Cupressus arizonica, 100
  cashmeriana, 145
  funebris, 57
  macrocarpa, 22, 28, 47, 94, 112, 119, 134
  recurva coxii, 64
  torulosa, 28
Cyathea, 141
Cyclamen, 146
  neapolitanum, 14, 30, 38, 49, 77, 80
  repandum, 54, 55, 62
Cytisus, 140
  battandieri, 96, 101
  X praecox, 76

Dacrydium franklinii, 64
Dahlia, 'Bishop of Llandaff', 104
Dartington Hall, garden at, 16, 33
Dasylirion acrotrichum, 138
Datura, 117
  sanguinea, 131
Davidia involucrata, 27, 38, 55, 86, 95, 97, 100, 112, 114, 143
Dendromecon rigida, 68, 131
Dianella, 103
Dicksonia antarctica, 16, 100, 141
Dillistone, Mr. George, 29
Dimorphotheca, 67, 140
  'Tresco Peggy', 140
Diplacus (Mimulus) glutinosus, 67
Dodonaea viscosa, 66, 128
Doreanthes palmeri, 140
Dorrien Smith, Lieut. Algernon, 135
Dorrien Smith, Major A.A., 135
Dorrien Smith, Mr. R.A., 17, 134
Dorrien Smith, Lt. Cdr. T.A., 138
Douglas, David, 33, 110
Drewe, Mr. Julius, Mr. Anthony, Dr. Christopher, Mr. Basil, 29

Drimys, 100
  laneolata, 95
  winteri, 47, 80, 95, 99
    var. *latifolia*, 87

Echium, 79, 102, 140, 146
  fastuosum, 140
  scilloniensis, 140
  'Tresco Blue', 140
  wildpretti, 140
Edgeworthia papyrifera, 94
Eleagnus, 77
  X *ebbingei*, 49, 72
Elmhirst, Dorothy and Leonard, 36, 39
Elwes & Henry, "The Trees of Great
  Britain", 26
Embothrium, 67, 73. 97, 114, 130, 145
  coccineum, 16, 47, 99
    'Norquinco Valley', 126
Emmenopterys henryi, 90
Endsleigh, garden and arboretum at,
  39, Figs. 5, 6, 7
Enkianthus, 30
  chinensis, 145
Erica arborea alpina, 37, 69
  canaliculata, 128
  diaphana, 138
  X *veitchii*, 51
    'W.T. Rackcliff', 96
Eriogonum giganteum, 139
Erythrina crista-galli, 117
Erythronium revolutum, 52, Pl. 3
    'White Beauty', 62, 68, 82
Escallonia macrantha, 14
  montevidensis, 147
Eucalyptus, 68, 98
  delegatensis, 94
  ficifolia, 138, 141, Pl. 5
  gigantea, 55
  glaucescens, 47, 73
  gunnii, 41, 73, 126
  nicholsii, 93
  niphophila, 47
  nitens, 47
  perriniana, 73
  regnans, 94
  viminalis, 72
Eucryphia, 15, 39, 67. 123
  billardieri, 146
  cordifolia, 26, 46, 56, 76, 114, 128,
    132, 144, 146
  glutinosa, 30, 42, 76
  X *intermedia*, 100
  lucida, 127
    X *cordifolia*, 52
  milleganii, 127
  moorei, 114, 127
  X *nymansensis*, 26
    'Nymansay', 31, 46, 52, 100

Euryops acraeus, 62, 73
Euonymus alatus, 37
  fortunei 'Variegatum', 123
Eupatorium ligustrinum, 31, 47
Euphorbia characias, 96
Euptelea pleiosperma, 145
Exbury, garden at, 86, 122

Fabiana imbricata, 118, 147
Fagopyrum, 22
Fagus sylvatica 'Pendula', 43
Farrand, Beatrix, 39
Farrer, Reginald, 88
Fascicularia bicolor, 67, 102, 116
Feesey, Mr. & Mrs. Mervyn, 147
Feijoa sellowiana, 47, 102, 117, 147
Fir, Douglas, 28
Fitzroya, 44
  cupressoides, 57
  patagonica, 74
Flete, garden at, 45
Forrest, George, 13, 88, 94, 127
Fortescue, L.S., 17, 48, 51
Fortescue, The Lady Margaret, 17, 31
Fothergilla, 39
Fox, Mrs. 17, 99
Fox, Alfred Esq., 99
Fox, Mr. Barclay, 100, 122
Fox, Cuthbert Esq., 99
Fox, Mrs. J.M.K., 113
Fox, Philip Esq., 99
Fraxinus, 22
  excelsior 'Aurea', 97
Fremontodendron californicum, 129
Fritillaria meleagris, 52
Fuchsia, 98, 101, 118
  excorticata, 80, 128
  magellanica, 14
Furcraea, 15, 139

Gardenia, 26
Garrya elliptica, 30, 103
Gazania, 67, 140
Genista cinerea, 49
Geranium 'Ballerina', 62
  maderense, 141
  palmatum, 141
  sanguineum var. *lancastriense*, 62
Gibson, Mr., 86
Ginkgo biloba, 36, 55, 82, 92
Glendurgan, garden at, 17, 99, Figs.
  22, 23
Grape Fruit Tree, 47
Grevillea rosmarinifolia, 79
  sulphurea, 118
Grewia sutherlandii, 140
Griselinia, 117
  littoralis, 131, 143
Gunnera, 93, 115

Hadden, Norman, 72
Halesia carolina, 32, 76, 94, 119
    monticola vestita, 32
Hare, Mr. & Mrs. E.H., 81
Harrison, General Eric, 15, 120
Harrison, Mrs. Rosa, 93
Hartia sinensis, 90
Heather, 98
Hebe, 14, 36, 74, 103, 108, 147
    'Amy, 67
    fairchildi, 118
    veitchii, 119
Helianthemum, 58
Helichrysum angustifolium, 103
    retortum, 62
    serotinum, 103
Helleborus corsicus, 110
    orientalis, 63, 79
Hemerocallis, 32, 37, 49, 87, 110
Hesperoyucca whipplei, 118
Hibiscus sino-syriacus, 49
Hickson, Michael, 63, 65
Hoblyn, Mrs. J.D. Peter, 105
Hoheria glabrata, 49
Hoheria lyallii, 30, 132
Holland, John, The Duke of Exeter, 37
Holman, Mr. & Mrs. Nigel, 17, 93
Hooker, J., 13, 91, 111, 133
Horder, Mr. Peter, 134
Hosta, 68
Hydrangea, 14, 38, 98, 101, 109, 117, 119, 123, 133, 144
    aspera, 63
    'Bluewave', 38
    petiolaris, 45, 97, 122
    quercifolia, 77, 80, 118
    sargentiana, 103
    scandens, 92
    villosa, 38, 97, 103
Hypericum calycinum, 96
    'Rowallane', 101, 133

Ilex dipyrenia, 22
Illicium anisatum, 77
Ince Castle, garden at, 102
Iris, 111
    attica, 73
    innominata, 82
Iveagh, Lord, 103

Jasminum mesnyi, 96
    polyanthum, 70, 116
Johnstone, Mrs. George, 17, 142
Johnstone, Mr. G.H., OBE, VMH, 142
Juniperus chinensis, 28, 41, 112
    recurva, 112
    sheppardii, 41
    'Sky Rocket', 66

Kalmia, 109
Kalopanax pictus, 43
Killerton, garden at, 53, Figs. 10, 11
Kingdon Ward, F., 13, 32, 53, 88, 126, 144
Knightshayes, garden at, 13, 17, 58, Figs. 12, 13, Pl. 3
Kniphofia, 110, 116
    roopiae, 116
Koelreuteria paniculata, 63, 104

Lagerstroemia indica, 45
Lamellen, garden at, 105, 121, Fig. 24
Lanarth, garden at, 127
Lanhydrock House, garden at, 107, Fig. 26
Lantana, 26
Lapageria rosea, 51, 117, 131
Lardizabala biternata, 47
Lavender, 58
Lees, Mrs. Mary, 146
Lemon, Sir Charles, 91
Le Nôtre, 23
Leonotis leonurus, 104, 116
Leptospermum, 26, 102, 103
    flavescens, 94
    scoparium, 51, 127
Lespedeza thunbergii, 103
Leucanthemum hosmariense, 62
Leucodendron argenteum, 139
    decorum, 139
    discolor, 139
Leucospermum, 139
Lewisea, 67
Lilium auratum 'Pink Glory', 31
    parkmanni, 46
    henryi, 46
    martagon, 64
    speciosum, 31, 147
Lindera megaphylla, 90
Liquidambar styraciflua, 39, 46
Liriodendron tulipifera, 100
Lithocarpus pachyphylla, 90
Lobb, William, 13, 47, 110, 113
Lobelia fulgens, 46, 103
    gibberoa, 141
    tupa, 67, 102
Lole, Mr. E.F., 93
Lucombe Oak, 91, 77
Luculia gratissima, 128
Ludlow, Frank, 32, 86
Lutyens, Sir Edwin, 29
Lysichitum, 93, 133

Macartney, Lord, 111
Magnolia 'Alba Superba', 96
    'Caerhays Surprise', 89

Magnolia (cont.)
campbellii, 13, 26, 38, 53, 54, 72,
    78, 82, 86, 88, 94, 103, 106,
    109, 111, 114, 127, 143, 146,
    Fig. 16, Pl. 1
  alba, 86, 94
  mollicomata 'Lanarth', 30, 86, 127,
    144
  'Charles Coates', 126
cylindrica, 54, 94, 105, 128, 143
dawsoniana, 30, 54, 86, 88, 94, 109,
    144
  'Chyverton', 94
delavayi, 38, 46, 77, 89, 102, 106,
    114, 132
denudata, 38, 54, 87, 100, 109, 126,
    128, 129
fraseri, 54
globosa, 94, 106, 119, 128
grandiflora, 26, 46, 87, 96, 102,
    108, 111
  'Goliath', 36
X *highdownensis*, 129
hypoleuca, 38, 94, 109, 114, 128
'Kew's Surprise', 89
kobus, 53, 54, 108, Fig. 11
'Leonard Messel', 108
liliflora, 143
  'Nigra', 75
X *loebneri* 'Merrill', 66
macrophylla, 54
mollicomata, 89
    'Charles Raffill', 72, 86, 108,
      127, 132
    subsp *mollicomata*, 30, 86, 88,
      100, 132, 143, 146
nitida, 93, 128
rostrata, 89, 109, 133
salicifolia, 52
sargentiana, 114, 115
    X *mollicomata*, 95
    robusta, 38, 82, 86, 88, 94, 105,
      109, 131, 144, Fig. 4
    X *mollicomata*, 89
sieboldii, 54, 128
    X *tripetala*, 126
sinensis, 63, 89, 96
X *soulangiana*, 92, 94, 100, 108,
    112, 143
  'Lennei', 37, 46, 75, 82, 100, 109
  'Rustica Rubra', 96
sprengeri diva, 72, 82, 86, 88, 94,
    127, 144
    X *M. sargentiana robusta*, 89
stellata, 54, 94, 115, 130, 144
  rosea, 108
tripetala, 26
tsarongensis, 94
X *veitchii*, 38, 54, 79, 86, 87, 88,

Magnolia (cont.)
    108, 123, 126
  'Isca', 86, 109
  X *watsoni*, 39, 128
  wilsonii, 63, 89
Magor, Major E.W.M., 105
Mahonia, 92
  lomariifolia, 118
Maidwell Hall, garden at, 144
Malus baccata, 95
  hupehensis, 38, 95
Malva moschata, 49
Maranta, 26
Marwood Hill, garden at, 17, 65,
    Fig. 14
Maurandia erubescens, 66
Meconopsis, 133
  grandis, 32
Melaleuca hypericifolia, 128
Melianthus major, 104, 118
Mesembryanthemum, 14, 116, 140
Metasequoia glyptostroboides, 33, 100,
    112, 126
Metcombe Brake, garden at, 68
Metrosideros, 15
  robusta, 141
  tomentosa, 138, 141
Michelia, 89
  compressa, 127
  doltsopa, 86, 89, 94, 101, 109, 119,
    127, 128, 145
  excelsa, 127
Mildmay, Lord, 45
Mildmay, Lady, 46
Mimosa, 26
Mitchell, Alan, 26, 33, 43, 44, 54, 55,
    87, 105, 111, 112
Molesworth, Sir William Bt., 110
Molesworth-St. Aubyn, Lt. Col. J.A. &
    Mrs., 17, 111
Molesworth-St. Aubyn, Sir John Bt.,
    17, 112
Molesworth-St. Aubyn, The family of,
    110
Moore, Henry, 36, 37
Morley, Earl of, 75
Mulberry, Black, 45
Musa basjoo, 119, 140
Mutisia oligodon, 66, 68
Myosotidium hortensia, 63, 131
Myrtus communis, 45, 97
  lechlerana, 87, 114
  luma, 37, 76, 94, 116, 132, 140,
    Pl. 6

Narcissus eystettensis, 22
  'Scilly White', 135
  'Soleil d'Or', 135
Nasturtium, 104

National Trust, The, 21, 29, 53, 58,
  75, 76, 78, 85, 96, 99, 107, 109,
  110, 115, 118, 123, 147
Nerine, 22
  bowdenii, 38, 76
  sarniensis, 117
Newell, Mr. John, 48
Newman, Lady A., 146
Nothofagus, 16, 55, 143
  menziesii, 90
  obliqua, 55, 90, 111
  procera, 90, 145
Nymans, garden at, 13, 108
Nyssa sylvatica, 27

Oak, Turkey, 102
Olearia, 74, 117
  albida, 14
  cunninghamii, 87
  forsteri, 131
  gunniana, 119
  paniculata, 131
  X *scilloniensis*, 130
  semi-dentata, 138
Ourisia coccinea, 72
Overbeck, Mr. Otto, 78
Oxydendrum, 37

Pachystegia insignis, 123
Paeonia, 110
  delavayi, 52, 79
  lutea ludlowii, 32
  mlokosewitschii, 73
Page, Russell, 46
Palmer, Colonel & the Lady Anne, 17, 71
Parrotia persica, 77, 123
Passiflora coerulea, 128
Passion Flower, 26
Paulownia imperialis, 129
  tomentosa, 92, 114, 129
Pelargonium, 15, 117, 139
  'Mabel Gray', 70
Pencarrow, garden at, 16, 110
Penjerrick, garden at, 15, 79, 113,
  122, Fig. 27
Phlomis fruticosa, 67, 92, 96
Phoenix canariensis, 139
Phormium tenax, 16, 49, 62, 67, 104
  'Purpureum', 80
  'Veitchii', 80
Photinia 'Red Robin', 32, 64
  X *fraseri*, 64
    'Birmingham', 119
    robusta, 64
    villosa, 37, 64
Picea abies, 43
  albertiana conica, 49
  brewerana, 57, 112
  jezoensis var. *hondoensis*, 44

Picea (cont.)
  omorika, 44
  orientalis, 44
  polita, 41, 44
  rubens, 44
  smithiana, 41, 107, 113, 119
Pieris floribunda, 69
  formosa, 92
    forrestii, 92, 94, 114, 142
  japonica, 76
Pine, Monterey, 28
Pinus armandii, 44, 113
  bungeana, 87
  coulteri, 28
  lambertiana, 28
  montezumae, 27, 40, 44, 112
  patula, 64, 94, 119, 129
  pinea, 77
  ponderosa, 28
  radiata, 14, 28, 37, 45, 77, 86, 106,
    111, 116, 119, 134, 147
  wallichiana, 44, 129
Pittosporum eugenioides, 80, 145
  tenuifolium, 14, 63, 74
    'Garnetti', 101, 119
    'Purpureum', 145
  tobira, 14, 128, 131
Podocarpus, 44
  andinus, 28
  chilensis, 115
  macrophyllus, 28
  nubigenus, 28, 112
  salignus, 27, 28, 95, 97, 112
  totara, 105
Polyanthus, Barnhaven, 82
Polygonum, 22
Potentilla, 147
  fruticosa, 36, 37, 97
    'Primrose Beauty', 97
Powys, Sidmouth, garden at, 69
Primula denticulata, 32
  florindae, 133
    'Garryarde Guinevere', 74
  gracilipes, 63
  helodoxa, 100, 133
  japonica, 133
  prolifera, 133
Prostanthera rotundifolia, 118
Protea barbigera, 139
  compacta, 139
  cynaroides, 139
Prunus 'Amanogawa', 92
  'Kanzan', 100
  'Kursar', 71
  sargentii, 69
  serrula, 74
  'Shirofugen', 94
  'Tai-Haku', 36, 100
  yedoensis, 72

Pseudotsuga menziesii, 41
Pterocarya fraxinifolia, 112
    stenoptera, 112
Puya alpestris, 140
    berteroniana, 140
    chilensis, 140
Pyrus salicifolia pendula, 62

Quercus acuta, 28
    borealis, 55
    canariensis (mirbeckii), 55
    hispanica 'Lucombeana', 38
    ilex, 38, 55, 75, 135
        latifolia, 21
    laevigata, 55
    lamellosus, 90
    myrsinaefolia, 28
    petraea, 65
    phellos, 28, 101
    pubescens, 95
    robur, 65
    suber, 55, 70, 87, 104, 146, Fig. 10
    velutina, 90

Raffill, C.P., 89
Rapalostylis sapoa, 141
Raphiolepis umbellata, 129
Rehderodendron macrocarpum, 144
Repton, Humphry, 40
Rhododendron aberconwayi, 30
    albrechtii, 69, 132
    'Alison Johnstone', 122, 143
    'Altaclarense', 21
    anwheiense, 94
    'Apple Blossom', 87, 114
    araiophyllum, 91
    arboreum, 42, 54, 56, 77, 108, 121,
        130, 132, 133
        'Red Admiral', 89
        forma roseum, 56
        'Sir Charles Lemon', 51, 91
        subsp. *cambelliae*, 56
        subsp. *cinnamomeum*, 56
    arizelum, 56, 94, 126
    'Arnia', 121
    'Arthur Osborn', 30
    'Assaye', 90
    augustinii, 69, 87, 93, 100, 105,
        114, 119, 121
        X *caeruleum album*, 122
        X *impeditum*, 106
    'Avalanche Alpine Glow', 67
    barbatum, 121, 130
    'Barclayi', 122
        'Helen Fox', 100
    'Beatrice', 122
    'Beauty of Tremough', 100
    'Belle of Tremeer', 122
    'Blue Star', 121

Rhododendron (cont.)
    'Bow Bells', 32
    burmanicum, 143
        'Lanarth', 94
    'Caerhays John', 89
    'Caerhays Philip', 51, 89
    'Calfort', 72
    callimorphum, 121
    calophytum, 72, 107, 133
    campanulatum, 56
    campylocarpum, 97, 130
        elatum X *griffithianum*, 51
    carolinianum hybrids, 106
    caucasicum, 42
    chamaethomsonii, 63
    'Charles Michael', 94
    'Chikor', 73
    'Chink', 73
    chrysodoron, 128, 143
    'Chrysomanicum', 143
    ciliatum, 56
    ciliicalyx, 106
    cinnabarinum roylei, 93, 114
    'Clio', 107
    concatenans, 121, 143
        X *R. cinnabarinum*, 51
    concinnum var. *pseudoyanthinum*, 121
    'Conyan', 121
    coriaceum, 56
    'Cornish Cross', 15, 113, 115
    'Cornish Red', 91, 93, 95, 105, 108,
        130
    crassum, 90, 100
    crebreflorum, 51
    'Crest', 72
    cubittii, 70
    'Curlew', 73
    'Cynthia', 109
    'Damaris', 106
    davidsonianum, 114
    delavayi, 56
    'Dr. Stocker', 56, 122
    eclecteum, 57
    edgeworthii, 94
        X *moupinense*, 123
    'Edmondi', 121
    'Elizabeth', 51, 122, 129
    elliottii, 126
    'Endsleigh Pink', 42
    eximimium, 92
    falconeri, 23, 91, 112, 132, Figs. 19,
        28
        X *R. lacteum*, 89
        X *R. macabeanum*, 89
    'Fortune', 122
    fortunei, 72, 107
    X *fragrantissimum*, 15, 92, 106
    'Full House', 143
    fulvum, 56

Rhododendron (cont.)
'Fusilier', 130
'Gauntletti', 106
'George Johnstone', 143
giganteum, 86, 115
    X *magnificum*, 95
'Gilian', 106
'Gill's Goliath', 92
glaucophyllum luteiflorum, 32
'Gloria Mundi', 57
'Golden Oriole Talavera', 90, 132
grande, 130
griersonianum, 51, 95, 130
griffithianum, 51, 85, 91, 133
'Hermione', 107
'Hinodegiri', 114, 118, 130
'Hinomayo', 114, 130
hodgsonii, 56, 122
houlstonii, 107
impeditum, 120, 121, 131
irroratum, 107, 122
'Jack Skelton', 51, 145
'John Barr Stevenson', 122
'Johnnie Johnston', 133
johnstoneanum, 57, 63, 133
'Katharine Fortescue', 51
lacteum, 121
    X 'Damaris Logan', 122
'Lady Alice Fitzwilliam', 15, 38, 90, 114, 130
'Lady Berry', 52
'Lady Chamberlain', 52, 76, 119
'Lady Rosebery', 52
'Lamellen', 106, Fig. 24
lanigerum, 133
lapponicum, 73, 131
lindleyi, 15, 86, 145
    X *sino-nuttallii*, 128
'Lionel's Triumph', 122
'Loderi', 76, 77, 109
Loderi 'King George', 38, 69, 100, 114
Loderi 'Pink Diamond', 114
Loderi 'Sir Edmund' X *wardii*, 122
'Luscombei', 121
lutescens, 22, 69, 87
luteum, 86
lyi, 106
macabeanum, 13, 86, 95, 106, 112, 122, 126, 130, 133, 144, Fig. 31, Pl. 7
    X *magnificum*, 94
    X *sinogrande*, 95
maddeni, 15, 51, 89, 106, 129, 130, 132
    sect., 15
'Maestro', 122
magnificum, 133
magorianum, 107

Rhododendron (cont.)
mallotum, 130
'Marcia', 52, 93
'Mariloo', 122
'Mars', 109
'Matador X Gaul', 122
megacalyx, 132
'Michael's Pride', 89, 145
mollicomum, 106
mollyanum, 105, 122
'Morvah', 126
moupinense, 63
'Mrs. Kingsmill', 106
mucronatum, 126
mucronulatum, 106
'Mystic', 122
neriiflorum, 106, 130
'Nobleanum', 30
nuttallii, 15
obtusum 'Amoenum', 126
orbiculare, 69
    X *R. decorum*, 90
'Oreocinn', 107
oreotrephes, 69
'Palestrina', 38
'Peace', 122
'Penjerrick', 15, 51, 100, 106, 113, 114
'Penjerrick Cream', 119
'Penjerrick White', 119
'Pensive', 122
'Pink Pebble', 121
'Pipaluk', 122
'Polar Bear', 31
polyandrum, 119
polylepis, 57
ponticum, 21, 42
X *praecox*, 130
praestans, 56
'Queen Elizabeth II', 51
quinquefolium, 93
racemosum, 73
'Red Admiral', 15
'Red Fortunei' X 'Laura Aberconway', 122
rex
rhabdotum, 130, 143
'Robert Keir', 121
'Romany Chal', 52
'Roza Stevenson', 122
rubiginosum, 56
russatum, 72, 121
'Russautinii', 52
'Saffron Queen', 100
'St. Breward', 15, 105, 121
'St. Merryan', 121
'St. Minver', 15, 121
'St. Tudy', 15, 121
saluenense, 49, 73, 121, 131

Rhododendron (cont.)
  'Sappho', 42
  scabrifolium, 106
  schlippenbachii, 93, 130, 132
  scintillans, 131
  scopulorum, 106
  'Shilsonii', 130
  simsii, 70
  sinogrande, 77, 86, 89, 95, 104, 115,
    122, 133
    boreale, 130
  spiciferum, 72
  stamineum, 90, 132
  stenaulum, 132
  sulfureum, 106
  taggianum, 15, 132
  'Tally Ho', 52
  'Temple Belle', 32
  tephropeplum, 133
  'Thomasine', 72
  thomsonii, 22, 82, 130
  'Tretawn', 107
  'Trewithen Orange', 143
  triflorum, 87
  tsariense, 121
  'Tyermannii', 15, 106
  vaseyi, 30, 114
  'Velaspis', 132
  venator, 56
  viscosum, 27
  wardii 'Ellestee' X 'Windsor Hawk', 51
  wattii, 126
  williamsianum, 49, 90, 121
    X *R. callimorphum*, 90
    hybrids, 32, 38, Pl. 2
  yakusimanum, 73, 106, 121
  'Yellow Hammer', 89
  'Yum Yum', 121
  yunnanense, 30, 56, 86, 130
  zeylanicum X *griffithianum*, 90
  'Zyxya', 122
Rhus, 39
  trichocarpa, 119
Robartes, Lord, 107
Robinia 'Frisia', 102
Romneya, 92
Romulea bulbocodium, 62
Rosa, 98, 111
  alba 'Celeste', 73
  X *anemonoides* 'Ramona', 92
  banksiae, 71, 97
  bracteata, 111, 118, 147
  filipes, 75
  hugonis, 39
  moyesii, 39
  omeiensis 'Pteracantha', 30
  paulii, 73
  primula, 39
  rugosa, 103, 116

Rose 'Golden Wings', 119
  'Iceberg', 87
  'La Mortola', 103
  'Maréchal Niel', 82
  'Mermaid', 36, 47
Rosemary, 74
Rosemoor, garden at, 17, 71
Royal Horticultural Society, The, 110,
  120, 126, 142
Rubia peregrina, 81
Rue, 75
  'Jackman's Blue', 33

Sage, 103
St. Aubyn, The Hon. J.F., 17, 115
St. Levan, Lord, 115
St. Michael's Mount, garden at, 115
Salix hastata 'Wehrhahnii', 67, 72
Saltram, garden at, 75, Fig. 15
Salvia grahamii, 104
  uliginosa, 67
Sampford, Mr. & Mrs. Anthony, 32
Santolina, 58
Savill Garden, Windsor, 13, 73, 105,
  106
Saxegothea conspicua, 57
Saxifraga grandiflora, 114
Schima argentea, 127
  khasiana, 94, 132, 144
Schizandra rubrifolia, 96
Schizostylis coccinea, 30
Sciadopitys veerticillata, 57
Scilla lilio-hyacinthus, 118
  mesanensis, 63
Sedum, 147
  'Ruby Glow', 103
  'Vera Jameson', 49
Sempervivum, 147
Senecio laxifolius, 36
  rotundifolius, 14
Sequoia sempervirens, 41, 76
Sequoiadendron giganteum, 43, 53
Sharpitor (Overbeck's), garden at, 78,
  Fig. 16, Pl. 1
Sherriff, Major George, 32, 86
Silley, Mr. Jack, 91
Slade, garden at, 81
Smart, Dr. J.A., 17, 65
Smith, Mr. Augustus, 134
Smith, Mr. S., 114, 115
Solanum crispum, 26, 36
Sollya drummondii, 92
Sophora microphylla, 58
  tetraptera, 70, 147
Sorbus 'Joseph Rock', 103
  matsumurana, 123
  'Mitchellii', 95
  vilmorinii, 104
Soukop, Willie, 36

Spartium junceum, 116
Spruce, sitka, 28, 32
 'Tiger-Tail', 113
Stachys lanata, 96
Stachyurus praecox, 63
Staphylaea colchica, 39, 75
 holocarpa rosea, 39
Staplers, garden at, 146
Stephanandra incisa, 70
Stewartia koreana, 39
 pseudocamellia, 39, 55, 106
 sinensis, 127, 145
Stourhead, 40
Streptosolen jamesonii, 26
Styrax hemsleyana, 128
 japonica, 42, 95, 127
 obassia, 42, 56, 93
Synge, Mrs. M.G., 17
Syringa microphylla, 82
 emodi 'Variegata', 80

Taiwania cryptomerioides (formosa), 57
Tamarix, 103
Tapeley Park, garden at, 146
Taxodium ascendens 'Nutans', 112
 distichum, 36, 46, 68
 'Pendulum', 100
Taxus, 44
Taylor, Mr. Michael, 145
Tetracentron sinense, 90
Teucrium, 36
 fruticans, 118
Thalictrum dipterocarpum, 49
 glaucum, 37
Thomas, John, 93
Thuja plicata, 41
 'Zebrina', 105
Thujopsis dolobrata, 26, 41, 44
Tibouchina semidecandra, 131
 urvilliana, 131
Tilia platyphyllos 'Laciniata', 40
 tomentosa, 47
Tithonia rotundifolia, 104
Torreya, 44
 grandis, 28
Tower Court, garden at, 120, 121, 122
Trachelospermum jasminoides, 36
Trachycarpus fortunei, 78, 147
Tregunna, Mr. Philip, 90
Trelissick, garden at, 14, 118
Tremayne, Captain Charles H., 92
Tremeer, garden at, 15, 120, Fig. 25
Trengwainton, garden at, 13, 14, 17, 106, 123, Fig. 28
Trerice, garden at, 147

Tresco Abbey, garden at, 13, 14, 102, 134, Fig. 29, Pls. 5, 6
Trewithen, garden at, 13, 14, 16, 17, 51, 70, 86, 99, 106, 122, 142, Figs. 30, 31, Pl. 7
Tricuspidaria lanceolata, 16
Trochodendron aralioides, 80
Tsuga heterophylla, 41
Tulipa saxatilis, 66
Tulip Tree, 54, 74, 87, 97, Fig. 23

Ulmus glabra 'Pendula', 43
 viminalis, 87
Underhill, Terry Mr., 39

Vaccinium retusum, 127, 145
Veitch, Mr. Robert, 53, 110
Venido-Arctotis, 140
Venidium, 140
Veratrum, 110
Verbascum, 37
Veronica persica, 21
Vestia lycioides, 118
Viburnum, 68, 102
 betulifolium, 14, 32, 144
 X *burkwoodii*, 74
 carlesii, 71
 X *chenaultii*, 49
 davidii, 30, 73, 92
 'Diane', 71
 X *juddii*, 62
 'Lanarth', 73
 odoratissimum, 80
 plicatum, 94
 plicatum tomentosum, 119
 rhytidophyllum, 96
Vitis, 36

Wakehurst, garden at, 13
Wallich, N., 111
Watsonia, 66, 70, 117, 139
Weekes, Mr. & Mrs. H.F., 68
Weinmannia trichosperma, 64, 128
Williams, F. Julian Esq., 88
Williams, J.C. Esq., 88
Wilson, E.H., 88, 90, 107, 120
Wisteria, 22, 111, 118, 142
 floribunda 'Macrobotrys', 119
Woodside, Barnstaple, garden at, 147
Wyatville, James, 40

Yucca, 58, 75, 110
 gloriosa, 80

Zelkova carpinifolia, 28
 crenata, 29